LONG LESSONS

Hannah,

So glad that you visited us! Please come back soon!

[signature]

LONG LESSONS

What I Thought I Knew about (Wiener) Dogs

A Memoir

by

Jason A. Garrison

Long Lessons
by Jason A. Garrison

ISBN-10: 0991084217
ISBN-13: 978-0-9910842-1-0

Published by
J. A. Garrison
Memphis, Tennessee

Although the incidents in this work are substantially as I
remember them, the names and certain identifying features
of some people portrayed in it have been changed to protect
their privacy. – Jason Garrison

www.jagarrison.com

TABLE OF CONTENTS

Preface..vii

Small Dogs Aren't Tough 1

Tiny Dogs Are for Wimps...........................11

All Lap Dogs Are Cuddly 23

Wiener Dogs Are Fat....................................34

He'll Learn It All in No Time 46

Grooming Is a Breeze...................................56

Losing Those Is Not a Good Idea................64

They Share and Share Alike.........................72

He's a Natural Guard Dog............................80

He's Fine by Himself 89

He Loves Us Both the Same 99

A Neutered Dog Has No Passion 110

They Are Picky Eaters................................120

They Won't Take Pills 128

Three Is Too Many.....................................137

A Female Won't Be Different.....................144

She's Either a Chicken or a Shar Pei.........153

He Can't Reach It.......................................162

They Aren't Interested in Clothes 172

The Others Are Immune.............................181

It's Just a Dog...!..191

Sparky Is the Alpha 201

We'll Have to Put Him Down 209

No One Wants a Stray 221

They'll Live Forever 232

Notes 238

PREFACE

I was wrong. There, I said it. I figure we should just go ahead and get that out of the way since this whole book covers just about all of my misconceptions about dogs.

Having been a student, scholar, and educator for several years, I always take great pride in getting things right. Heck, I've been known to verify things in two or three sources before I confirm something publically; and even then I'm worried that I might be wrong about some fact, date, or name. So describing how I was wrong in every chapter of this book isn't easy, though it's probably good for my ego.

Since I've spent most of my adult years ensconced in the academic side of theological and religious studies, I can't tell you how many strange looks I get from folks when I tell them that I've been writing a book about weenie dogs. Some of their faces contort a little as they try to riddle out how weenie dogs have some relationship to church doctrines or philosophical concepts. But I assure you I have no religious axe to grind in this book. It's just a fun and hopefully inspiring story that I've wanted to tell for years about the nutty stuff my dogs do and some of the lessons I learned along the way.

Since this book is a rather peculiar project for me, I wanted to give some preliminary statements before we begin:

~*Wiener is in parentheses*. You'll notice from the title *Long Lessons: What I Thought I Knew about (Wiener) Dogs* that *wiener* is in parentheses. That's because most of the lessons I learned came from the Dachshunds I would eventually own, but I learned some other things from different dogs I encountered along the way. I could have just made the subtitle *What I Thought I Knew about Dogs*, but it didn't seem right since most of my stories come from weenie dogs. Plus, *Long Lessons* works better because it has to do with long dogs. And let me just tell you something, figuring out a good title for a book can be hard work! I went through a dozen different possibilities like *In the Long Run* or *The Lengths We Go* before I could land on a good one. I even thought about *The Man with Three Weenies*, but felt it was misleading.

~*Each chapter title is my own misconception about dogs.* I used to think dogs were pretty simple: feed 'em, bathe 'em, take 'em out for a walk, and that's about it. But I was wrong about a lot of things. So when Chapter 1 states that "Small Dogs Aren't Tough," that's not exactly true. In fact, each chapter title in this book represents one of my misconceptions, and the events described in the chapter will prove me wrong.

~*This book is an imperfect memoir.* I've done my best to verify information, but I'm sure I'll still get some things wrong. If you're looking for a book on how to raise, housetrain, or choose the right dog, then you should probably find another book. You definitely don't want to take advice from an author who proves to be wrong in every single chapter. Furthermore, I've changed the names and descriptions of many of the folks portrayed in the book to protect their privacy.

~*There is no secret agenda.* "Hey, wait a minute," you may be thinking. "This writer is a religious scholar? I'll bet he's gonna try to convert me or something." Nope. I'm not interested in anything like that. You *will* see me talk about the Bible and other ancient texts here and there, but they are only my unobtrusive reflections. If at any time you feel like I'm being preachy, just remind yourself that you're reading a book about weenie dogs and continue on. Besides, a book that mentions poop as much as this one can't be all that serious.

Finally, I'd like to thank all the people who have encouraged me to write, including my family: Mom, Dad, Lance, Todd, Julia, Norma, Heather, Kevin, and Kane. Herb, Wes, and Matthew were also a great encouragement. I'd like to thank Dale for advising me on the cover art, and Evonne, Heather, Cory, Ashley, and Devlin for their reflections on the manuscript. Lots of people have encouraged me along the way; I wish I could name you all.

But without question, Allyson has been an indispensable part of this book, and the most precious part of my life. Her unwavering belief in me has constantly motivated me to do my best. Though I have worked with language and rhetoric for many years, when it comes to my love for her, words fail me. But maybe these will do: I love you very much.

SMALL DOGS AREN'T TOUGH

Lap dogs aren't real dogs. At least that's what I came to believe while I was growing up. My parents raised my two brothers and me in the country, the heart of Alabama. We lived in Oak Grove, a small town with a single two-lane road running through a heavily wooded rural area with one school, one convenience store, and one church. If someone said they were going to the store, we knew what they meant. If someone said they'd meet you at the church, the Baptist church was the only one around. It was a small and wonderful community.

The country boys who lived there were into hunting, fishing, and farming; and just about all of them had dogs that took part in their adventures. Not one of them was a lap dog with a bow on its head. Instead, they had to be big enough to manage the rural environment. The hunters liked to take their retrievers with them to the local outdoorsmen clubs. I attended some of these with my dad when I was a kid, learning how to hunt, fish, and camp. I also got to know the dogs that were always a part of these trips. Some of them were well trained for duck hunting. On command, they'd swim across a lake to bring back a shot duck wherever it landed. But most of them weren't purebreds of any sort. Guys just wanted to bring their dogs with them, and they were always a great addition to the trip. In the country, it seemed that men just needed a dog as a companion. "Dogs are man's best friend," was a mantra that I clearly understood. Equally clear was the idea that dogs were just dogs. They were owned, not really adopted.

By the time I was a teenager, my parents separated and my dad moved even further into the country where he could plant his own farm—a hobby of his. Of course, he had a few dogs along the way.

One of them was an Australian Shepherd that lived about 14 years. He named her Matilda after the popular Australian song "Waltzing Matilda," and she was a very smart dog eager to please my dad. Her soft fur was thick and bushy, making a patchy black and white pattern down to her feet. Her legs were a light brown until they met her paws, which looked like she wore white anklet socks. Half of her friendly face was black contrasting the white and grey side. One eye was brown and the other was a sky blue. Her gorgeous face wore a perpetual grin. She was great for keeping foxes out of the chicken coop and alerted us if anyone was coming up the long driveway. She was friendly to those she knew but always stood between us and any suspicious visitors.

Then there was the other dog, Moes, a hound mixed with other breeds. His head almost reached the average person's waist, which made him a little taller than Matilda. He had a face that was longer than usual and a big snout that he had at the ground all of the time. With short, coarse fur that made no distinct black and white pattern, he wasn't much to look at. The hound in him was apparent since he was always finding some kind of trail, which often led to something that he would eat. It may not be food, but he would eat it just the same.

My mother-in-law made her feelings about Moes clear: he was the stupidest dog on the planet. It was hard to deny when I saw him chewing on a rock that he held upright between his paws. Rocks were one of his favorite delicacies, which I'm sure caused howling bowel movements. But I might also find him on the compost heap eating a softer snack of eggshells and slimy decomposed carrots. Or maybe he got into the trash and began working on the old milk carton holding a treasure of curdled milk inside. Not much of a guard dog, I think he broke into the chicken coop more than once, and I'm pretty sure he nabbed one of the big fancy goldfish out of my mother-in-law's pond. I'm surprised he lived through that one.

But my dad always defended Moes, insisting that he was a very smart dog. I'm not sure he believed that or if he was just trying to keep Moes alive. He tried fencing Moes up more than once, but the dog always found a way out—usually by force. If Moes had one thing going for him, it was his strength. You see, my dad had reasons for admiring and keeping Moes even though he was a problem sometimes. We country boys would come up with reasons for keeping our dogs. We loved them, were proud of them, and I think that we all identified with them on some level. It's another reason I couldn't take frail little lap dogs seriously. No one in my neighborhood did.

Eventually I graduated high school and went off to college at the University of Montevallo, a liberal arts school just south of Birmingham. While living on campus, I was more interested in meeting girls than hanging out with dogs. It was just as well, since no dogs were allowed on campus anyway. After college I roomed with a few friends in an apartment outside of Birmingham and started dating a hot young college student named Allyson.

Allyson was much smarter and more cultured than I. Her family had moved to several places around the Southeast during her childhood, which helped to develop her outgoing personality. She was working on her second degree at UAB when we met. She was so nice and pretty that I couldn't stop smiling around her. Later, she admitted that it was my bright, toothy smile that attracted her to me, which kept me brushing and flossing more than ever those days.

Things got serious quickly for us. Her mom and dad thought I was a good catch, and my mom said the same about Allyson. Not long after that, she and I met my dad and stepmother in town for lunch. We had such a great time, Dad invited us both over for dinner at his house the following week. Allyson agreed to the trip and was excited about getting to know my family better.

Dad lived about an hour's drive outside of town, so Allyson and I made it a point to leave earlier than usual. It gave us plenty of time to take the long road to his house so I could show her the countryside and the parts of Alabama she had never seen before. I took her past the house I lived in as a boy, the store, the church, and my school. On the way I told her what she could expect to see at my dad's house. He purchased several acres of undeveloped land in a solitary place between two hills. It was almost a valley with a few lakes and ponds less than a mile away, which made for good fishing. My dad had taken years to develop the land into his own little paradise with farmland, flowers, and even a few dogs.

"Dogs? What kind does he have?" Allyson asked. It was pretty clear what interested her the most about my description.

"He's had several over the years," I said. "But right now he has two."

After telling her about the graceful Matilda and Moes the rock eater, she really perked up. "I love dogs! We had three of them when I grew up: Snowball, Suki, and B.J. Snowball was a Pekinese-Poodle mix. Looked just like a snowball, all fat and fluffy. He was my sister's dog. I was in elementary school when I chose Suki as a little puppy. He was the littlest one in the litter. A Cockapeekapoo! A Cocker Spaniel, Pekingese, and Poodle mix. I named him Suki because I was in gymnastics and working on a maneuver called the Tsukahara. But B.J. was the dog we got before any of the others. He was a little brown Yorkshire Terrier. Our family got him when he was a puppy. We loved him to death! Funny thing is, he only had three legs."

I couldn't help but laugh. "Three legs? Why would you buy a three-legged dog?"

"Well, he wasn't like that when we bought him. He was this little puppy with this cute little nose!" Allyson's voice got a lot higher when talking about small dogs. Her hands came up holding the imaginary dog's face to hers as she cooed. I was getting the picture. Dogs were high on Allyson's list.

"We had a fenced-in back yard in Florida where we kept B.J. and Suki. We didn't have Snowball yet," she said. "Every now and then a neighbor would come by to visit us through the back gate. Only salesmen visited the front door. You know how it is. Somebody must have left the gate open, and that's when B.J. and Suki got out to roam the neighborhood.

"A few hours later we got a call from a neighbor several blocks away. She said that Suki came up to her barking frantically. She followed Suki into her garage. The door was open and there was B.J. in a pool of blood but still breathing. She found our info on the dog tags and called us. We took both the dogs to the vet. Suki was fine, but another dog had mauled B.J. The vet said from the look of it, a bigger dog bit him and shook him all over the place. He had some puncture wounds and was missing a lot of fur. We all thought it must have been Rex, a German Shepherd who lived up just up the hill that scared us all to death. If it wasn't for Suki, he'd have killed B.J. for sure."

"It's amazing that he was still alive!" I said. "He must have been a tough little guy. But losing a leg is a fair deal over dying!"

"He didn't lose the leg at first," she said. "We tried our best to keep it. The vet treated and wrapped it up, but B.J. kept licking at it. We'd go to school and come back to find it unwrapped and licked raw. We tried our best to treat it, but after a bad infection set in we had to have that leg amputated. But, you know, after he healed up, he was still just as active and happy as he was before. To him, it was as if nothing happened."

"Wow! He sounded like a tough little guy. Do you still own him?"

"No," said Allyson. "When Heather and I went to college, we left him with Mom. She was working long hours and felt bad leaving B.J. at home all day by himself. So she gave him away at a yard sale."

"Um …what?"

Allyson cried, "I know! Can you believe it? I was so mad at her! She had a yard sale one weekend while B.J. roamed around greeting all the guests. The cutest old couple looked through the stuff when they met B.J. and fell in love with him. They even asked if he was for sale. Mom thought it might be a good new home for B.J., but politely told them no and thought that was the end of it. But they came back within the hour with a new dog bed and some toys, and asked again if they could adopt B.J. That's when Mom decided that they could give him a better home with all the attention he deserved. So she gave them B.J. and all of his things for free. They were happy and so was he."

"So, how did you take it?" I asked.

"Not good! Even though she thought it was the right thing to do, she felt terrible about it and called me that night. I started crying and she started crying. But after we were cried out, it made sense to me. B.J. deserved a full-time family, and that's what he got. He'll be happy 'till the day he dies. It was hard on my sister too, but she came around. We still give Mom a hard time about the whole thing. The running joke is, 'You'd better behave when you're around her or she might give you away in a yard sale, too!'"

"Sounds like dogs have always been a big part of your life," I said.

Allyson nodded. "Well I'll tell you this, growing up I never really cared about being married or having kids, I just wanted a house with a big yard filled with dogs."

"And, where to you think that I fit in that picture?" I asked.

"I think a guy might be in the picture now."

"Fenced in the back yard?"

She laughed. "Playing with the dogs, yeah! But I might let you come inside…if you're a good boy."

The flirt batted her eyes at me. I gave her a toothy grin and drove a little faster. It was my teeth that nabbed this girl, after all.

****

When we pulled into my dad's driveway, the two dogs greeted us immediately. Matilda enjoyed a few strokes until Moes charged between us. Petting that slobbering lunatic was a challenge since he kept trying to slap his tongue all over my arms. I winced since I could only imagine where that thing had been. I glanced at Allyson who had just made a great new friend. She was scratching Matilda right behind the ears, her favorite spot. Matilda's eyes squinted and her hind leg started to kick.

"Don't let them jump on you," a deep voice advised. "They stink!" My dad greeted us from the back porch and invited us inside for a fine lunch and conversation about the property. He knew all the history about the undeveloped territory and was happy to tell us a few stories. After lunch, he took up our plates and moved to the kitchen sink where he continued to chat and wash the dishes. Occasionally, he gazed out the window just above the sink to survey his garden.

"Have you seen Granny lately?" I asked.

"No, I haven't seen her recently," Dad said while washing a plate. "I think it's been three days now. You know her. She'll show up out of the blue, visit for a little while, and then take off into the woods for days at a time."

Allyson looked bewildered. I could feel her stare at me when I asked, "She'll be gone for days? What does she do out there?"

"Oh, you know," Dad said plainly, still washing and staring. "She does whatever she pleases. I'll tell you, she *really* likes chasing after squirrels. One day she showed up with scratches all over her face, and a piece of her ear was torn off. She must have gotten ahold of a raccoon or something. But we patched her up and she took off into the woods again! She just loves it out there!"

Allyson was stoic. She either thought that she had seriously misunderstood the conversation, or that she needed to plot her escape from this mental institution in the middle of the woods. Hopefully she could avoid the crazy grandmother who probably had a dead squirrel hanging from her mouth that very moment.

With a giggle, I leaned over and said, "Grannie is the name of the neighbor's dog."

Allyson's head dropped in relief and began bobbing with laughter. "Whew! I didn't know what to think about your crazy grandmother chasing animals in the woods! I thought you all were out of your minds!"

Allyson made it through the little hazing event at my dad's house with no problem, which proved that she had a great sense of humor—a useful trait for those marrying into the Garrison household. Our relationship continued to grow over the next several months. We both liked each other and liked dogs. That was a good start.

TINY DOGS ARE FOR WIMPS

"Do you think we can get a dog?"

"No way."

We had been married a month when Allyson asked me what I thought about getting a dog—not a real dog, a little dog. Since we lived in the middle of Dallas in a small apartment, I didn't think it was a great idea regardless of the dog's size. And even the thought of being seen with a small dog turned me off completely. But if we didn't live in such a small space, I would have been open to some canine companionship, as long as it was a real dog that could at least climb up and down the stairs without assistance.

We were, after all, quite a distance from our families. Dallas was a ten-hour drive from my home in Birmingham and about an eighteen-hour drive from Allyson's family in North Carolina. It was a pretty big move that our families didn't appreciate as much, but was necessary for me to get the theological training I wanted. I had enrolled at Dallas Theological Seminary to pursue my dreams of becoming either a pastor or a theologian; I wasn't quite sure which, but was certain that there would be a lot of money in it (there wasn't). If not money, there had to be some fame (wrong again). If not fame, then at least personal fulfillment. Whatever the reason, I was drawn to the subject. While I was just beginning my studies, Allyson had just completed school to be an occupational therapist, but had a hard time finding work due to some big changes in healthcare.

School and work kept us busy most of the week, so I didn't think it was right to get a dog of any size. Allyson finally landed an entry-level job and was working all day while I was either at school or working sometimes late into the evening. But Allyson was the one who was home most of the time and was used to having a dog around. So we lived with the tension for a few months until something changed my mind.

Our closest friends at the time were Chuck and Amy who lived just a few miles away. Chuck and I knew each other at college before meeting again in Dallas. We first got acquainted at one of those social events at college and eventually roomed together for a few years. I wasn't interested in having a dog then either, but Chuck brought a puppy home one day that he named Molly. She was a beautiful brown German Shepherd with long legs, a narrow snout, and bushy tail. The dog grew fast, going from a few inches to a few feet in just a year. I can only imagine how much it cost Chuck in dog food.

At the time, we rented in a two-story townhouse, which had plenty of room out back where Chuck could walk and run Molly to exhaustion—his exhaustion. Molly, though, was unstoppable. They went out several times a day and all she would need was a leash and a tennis ball. Chuck walked her on the leash until they reached a clearing where he could throw the ball for about ten minutes. Then he'd hook her up and bring her back. From what I could tell, she was a low-maintenance dog: obedient, playful, and friendly.

Though harmless, her deep bark sounded like she could swallow a grown man whole, which made us feel pretty good about leaving the home unattended. She embodied all the traits I remembered about the dogs from my youth.

I moved out after graduation and didn't keep up with him and Molly. But years later when Allyson and I moved to Dallas, I was surprised to see that Chuck had also come to Dallas Seminary to get his own theological training. He married the girl he met in college, Amy, who he started dating just before I moved out of the townhouse. As we talked, he told me that Molly was no longer in the picture. She was such a big part of his life, one day I had to ask why she wasn't. He reminisced a little before explaining.

"Man, I really miss her. She was the best dog."

"Oh, I remember her," I said. "She was great! I thought you'd take her wherever you went. What happened?"

"You know how I would run her all the time in the field where we lived in college?" I nodded and he continued: "That's what she was used to, and I'd take her out there for a run every day. Man, she loved it. But when I decided to move to Dallas, I just didn't think that I'd have that same kind of space, you know? I figured we'd probably have to live in apartments or student housing for the first year or so until we could settle down. I couldn't let her stay cooped up like that; she was used to a bigger home with a yard. But my dad told me about one of his buddies who already had a dog and a great big yard. His friend was open to taking Molly, so we planned a visit.

"From the moment she got out of the car, she was happy. She loved the property, liked the other dog—a Chocolate Lab—and just adored the family. They had a little boy who threw the ball with both the dogs in that huge yard. Man...she was happy."

"So you ended up leaving her there?" I asked.

"Well, the plan was to visit the family first and see if Molly was a good fit, then drop her off just before we moved to Dallas. But Molly was like a fish in water. She loved it all. Even though I still had a little time before I had to move, I decided that it was best just to leave her there. The family was willing to take her right then, so...."

"Geez. That must have been tough to let her go," I said.

"It *was* tough. Before I left, I walked down the yard a bit, away from everyone, and played with her for like ten minutes." He sighed a little. "Then I scratched her behind the ears, thanked the family who took her and left with my dad. While we drove away she was still playing ball with the family. She was as happy as she could be. You know, I was such a baby about it; I cried when we left."

Chuck was a strong guy, so I was surprised he told me that. He grew up in the country like I did and guys like us didn't cry at the drop of a hat. I could tell that he really loved Molly. I knew her for a few months, but didn't really understand Chuck's kind of connection with her.

But when he and Amy moved to the city, they both felt like they needed a little company in their metro apartment. So after the first year there, they got another dog, a small brown and silver Yorkshire

Terrier. They named her Scrabble because of the way she darted back and forth across a room, scrambling things up I guess. They figured a smaller dog like her would be much more manageable in an apartment.

It was nice to see a familiar face at school, so Allyson and I made it a priority to meet with Chuck and Amy a few times over the next several weeks, and we eventually spent an evening with them at their home for a casual dinner and movie. That's when we got the chance to meet Scrabble the Yorkie in the flesh. In my mind, it was a pseudo-dog.

Chuck answered the door and welcomed us into his second floor apartment home. Inside we said hello to Amy who was getting our dinner ready, and then we greeted Scrabble. It was hard to miss her. She was yipping out a raspy bark and jumping around our feet. I think she was trying to scare us since we were new to her home. I wore the best fake-grin I could manage. As I said before, I was not a small-dog guy, and this was one of the reasons why. All the yipping was annoying and just too cute for a guy to really appreciate. I thought, *Chuck traded out Molly for this cream puff? Molly was a real dog! But this is just a rat! What was he thinking?*

It took a little time for Scrabble to get used to us, and she was especially afraid of me. I was the biggest person in the room, so I was the greatest threat I guess. When I ducked down to meet her, she scurried behind Chuck's feet with a shriek. Carefully she'd peek around his shins and cuss me out with her tiny shouts.

Ally, who had a way with dogs, sat down on the floor and started baby-talking to the little rodent, offering her open hand so Scrabble could sniff it. In less than a minute, Scrabble was on Allyson's lap soaking up all the attention with an occasional glance and growl in my direction.

"Well *fine* you little rat-dog! I didn't want to see you anyway!" I said. I was still grinning and everyone laughed, but I was halfway serious. This just helped seal the deal for me: tiny dogs were not my thing.

We all had a good time at dinner while Scrabble stayed in her small plastic kennel in the bedroom. She barked a little, but was quiet after a few minutes. After the spaghetti and salad, Chuck turned Scrabble lose and we all sat down in the living room to watch a movie. I was sitting next to Allyson in the love seat when Scrabble decided to spend some more time with her new friend. She jumped into Allyson's lap and soaked up all the attention until she fell soundly asleep. Allyson and I held hands through parts of the film, and before Scrabble and I knew it, I had my hand on the rat-dog's head. It was a little uncomfortable for both of us. I had never petted a rodent before, and Scrabble looked at me like I was a giant ape about to peel and eat a banana. But after a few minutes we learned that we could at least get along with each other. After the movie, I even got to throw Scrabble's ball with her a few times. The wall of hostility was down and by the end of the evening I thought she was all right...for a little rat-dog.

Allyson was sure that my exposure to Scrabble would make our need for a small dog clear, but I was unconvinced. Yeah, Scrabble was a neat dog, but a dog like that was not for me...I mean *us*. It would be too much trouble with all the yipping and jumping and ball chasing. It would be cute for only so long until it drove Allyson and I crazy. Plus, a dog like that was fragile. I'd probably step on her one day when I came home from work, or it might fall off the couch and land on its head.

I could envision the whole catastrophic event with amazing clarity. I'd come home from a day of work exhausted and sunburned, grab me a drink and collapse onto the couch in my slouched TV-watching posture, when I hear the muffled yelp of my new dog from somewhere beneath my posterior. Then I'd have to take the stupid thing to the vet and my nice relaxing evening would be ruined. After the whole ordeal, we'd be up to our eyeballs in vet bills.

Allyson may have been determined, but I wouldn't budge. A big dog was too much for us in an apartment, and a small dog was just a pain all around. And that was that. No dog for us until we could get a house. Looking back that was unrealistic since I would be in school for another few years and Allyson adored dogs. But I was stubborn and so was Allyson.

****

As Spring Break approached, people were making plans to go out of town to visit family or the beach. Money was tight for us, so Allyson and I decided to stay and work through the week. A few weeks earlier, Chuck gave me a call saying that he and Amy were going out of town for the break and needed someone to watch Scrabble. I wanted to help my buddy, but didn't want anything to do with his rat-dog, so I did what any friend would do: I hesitated and said I'd need to check with Allyson.

I was just blowing smoke. I knew Allyson would jump at the chance to keep Scrabble. They were the best of friends after all. Chuck agreed and when I spoke with Allyson that evening, she reacted happier than I thought she would. In fact, she was ecstatic. So we made plans to pick Scrabble up the night before they left.

When we brought Scrabble to our apartment, we had to make a few trips from the car. I was surprised how much equipment and chow the little rat required for just a week. She had a travel kennel where she slept at night, a separate pillow for napping during the day, her collar, a retractable leash, a roll of plastic poop bags, a satchel of toys, a bag of food with a precise measuring scoop, her own food bowl and big auto-feed water dish, a container of treats and a notepad delineating her routine, vet contact info and personal contact numbers for Chuck and Amy, with numbers for both of their parents for good measure. Sheesh! All this for a little furry muppet? I didn't get it. What I did get was the fresh roll of paper towels labeled "for mistakes" included in the supplies. "Great," I thought, "This probably means the whole apartment will smell like a toilet by the time she leaves."

When we finally got Scrabble and all her effects set up, we had a little fun. Allyson was more animated about it than I was. She said something like, "Well, Scrabble, welcome to the Garrison resort and weekend getaway!" I just rolled my eyes and played along.

For the next hour or so, we played with the little rat in the living room, going through all the toys she brought. A couple of squeaking animals with goofy faces, a squealing rubber hamburger, and a simple tennis ball matted with dried slobber were her favorite selections. I was surprised at how fast she chased each one of them when we hurled them across the room. I started telling myself that Scrabble wasn't such a bad dog to have around after all. Then again, I was sure she would pee on the floor before the night was over.

Dinner time followed playtime, and Allyson was eager to measure out the exact amount of kibble the notepad required. Scrabble recognized the sound of the food shaking around the bag and spun in several circles. That was her signature move. The more excited she got, the more she spun. She gobbled down her food in a flash and generously lapped up some of the fresh water we had just put out.

Since we were doing things by the book, the notepad said that Scrabble needed to go out immediately after each meal. Scrabble knew the routine and started spinning beside the front door. So Allyson and I hooked up the retractable leash to the collar, grabbed a poop bag and went out. We lived in a second floor apartment at the time with a long flight of metal and concrete stairs right outside the front door.

"Don't let her loose down the stairs," Allyson reminded me.

Oh right! She made a good point earlier that we need to make sure that the retractable leash didn't lock to a stop while Scrabble was halfway down the stairs. If the leash jerked, she could flip and hurt herself on the edge of a concrete step. I thought about that as the door opened a few inches. Scrabble didn't hesitate and tore down the stairs in a flash. "Holy Moses!" I yelled and ran down right behind her staggering over two and three steps at a time, I'm sure with the goofiest look of terror on my face. The leash just locked when Scrabble reached the bottom but she kept running, probably reacting to the thunderous commotion behind her. Allyson was as supportive as anyone should be. She was laughing so hard she made squeaks for breath and had to sit at the top of the steps.

I really didn't know how to drive that retractable leash thing, but I finally got the hang of it. If I needed to, I could reel Scrabble in like a fish; but most of the time I just let her roam on her own at the end of it. After exploring around the complex for a while, she did her business, I picked it up, and we headed back inside. By the end of the evening, Scrabble had decided that I was all right and fell asleep on my lap while I watched some TV. I was starting to grow fond of her, but I still found reasons not to like her. I wanted a dog with at least some semblance of toughness. I wanted a dog with backbone, and I hadn't seen that yet. She was cute, but I needed more than cute.

Through the week Scrabble and I spent a lot of time together. I did all the night walks with her and on one occasion she'd seen a squirrel and decided she was going to catch it come hell or high water. All cuteness gave way to a barking and snarling lunatic. When I first saw it, I laughed my head off. It was pretty cool to see that hunter side to Scrabble.

But what really floored me was when we crossed paths with a man walking his bigger dog. The Golden Retriever was friendly enough, but Scrabble didn't see him coming. When she did, her surprise put her into attack mode with all the snarling and barking again. I wasn't laughing this time and was shocked that she'd try to challenge a dog three times her size. The Retriever shrank back at all the aggression. After the moment passed, they cordially met and—you know—sniffed each other, which made everything fine again. Scrabble got along fine with dogs, but she didn't like to be surprised. In turn, I thought *This dog is tougher than I thought!*

When we got home, I looked up some information on Yorkshire Terriers, Scrabble's breed. Turns out, she really *was* a little rat dog! Yorkies were bred to hunt and kill rats in England. The fact that they were hunters made them much different from other lap dogs. I read that they were obedient and loyal to their masters. At the same time, they could be little terrors if intimidated. The more I read, the more of my stereotypes about Scrabble melted away. I remember reading some of the info with my mouth agape. I turned and looked at Scrabble resting comfortably on her pillow with half-destroyed chew toy lying next to her. I said, "Turns out that you're a mean little cuss when you want to be!" She simply glanced at me and laid her head back down. I swear she smiled at me, indifferent to the fluffy guts of the squeak toy strewn around her.

The end of that week actually came too quickly for me. I remember when we dropped Scrabble off that I actually missed the little rat-dog, and Allyson knew it. She went so far as to say that I actually loved the little rat. "No I don't!" I said in a very deep voice. Still, when I told her that I was reconsidering getting a dog, she was stoked.

To this day, I'm suspicious that she orchestrated the whole ordeal to make me change my mind about small dogs. I ask her about that from time to time, and she always denies it with a strange little smile.

ALL LAP DOGS ARE CUDDLY

Our search for a new dog began in the newspapers. Over the next few weeks we scanned the ads looking for any kind of small dog we could find. There were several dogs that needed a home. Lots of puppies from breeders. Lots of large dog breeds (dang it!). But several small dog options were available too. Since we were so partial to Scrabble, and since Allyson's former dog B.J. was a Yorkie, we spent most of our time looking for a Yorkshire Terrier of our own.

Since I was in school money was sparse, so we kept our eye out for good deals. One ad in particular caught Allyson's eye. It was a one-year old Yorkie that needed a new home. I called the number and heard a woman's voice on the other end. Her name was Katie Cane. She said that she and her husband were both professionals who worked long hours. They wanted their dog to have a home where he could be happy and get all the attention he deserved.

I explained that Allyson and I had adjusted our schedules to allow plenty of time for us to spend with our new dog. We both worked at different times which meant that we'd have to leave a dog at home only about five hours a day, and most weekends we spent at home. It sounded like a good arrangement for us all, so we got directions to the home and made plans to meet the Yorkie and his family.

We walked up the three flights of stairs to their apartment and knocked on the door, expecting to hear the happy accolades of a young dog. Instead we heard a maniacal screech mixed with hoarse barking getting closer and closer. Then—*Bam!*—the dog ran into the other side of the door just at our feet and didn't stop his tirade of barks and snarls, scratching wildly at the door. Allyson and I both looked a little freaked out. *Maybe we're at the wrong address.*

We heard a woman's voice draw near, "Tigger! Tigger! Calm down! Come here!" Then the unstable yipping faded. The door slowly opened and we met Mr. Cane.

The dog's reaction had already put us on edge, and Mr. Cane's appearance did not set us at ease. He was well dressed in professional attire but no tie, clean-shaven, and hair combed neatly to the side...and he was huge. Compared to *me* he was huge. At the time I was over six feet and weighed over two hundred pounds. I worked labor jobs, which kept me pretty strong. This man towered over me at nearly seven feet, putting his enormous pecks at my eye level.

He smiled, and welcomed me with an extended hand, "I guess you're the Garrisons!"

"Nice to meet you, Mr. Cane," I squeaked.

"Please, call me Groot." His voice was deep but pleasant. The handshake was uncomfortable, his giant fingers wrapping around my hand, thumb, and a little up my wrist. He gave me one good shake that knocked me off balance a little, and then invited us in.

When we walked into the living room, the frantic barking continued. Katie held a terrified little yipping machine that struggled to get lose. Tigger, I presumed.

We approached Tigger slowly using the sweetest voices that we could manage to say hello. Allyson exaggerated her smile and offered her hand for him to examine. Still in Katie's arms, he stared motionless at Allyson, growled a little and snapped at her.

"Tigger! That is not nice!" Katie said. "Bad dog!"

That's when I thought this might be a mistake, but Allyson kept up her sweet voice and kind words to the dog. "Maybe we should sit down so Tigger can get used to us," she said.

So we sat on their Italian leather couch and spent some time talking to the Canes. They both moved to Dallas for business and were executives who each worked about ten hours a day. Since they exercised regularly and had an active nightlife, they were hardly home and felt terrible for neglecting Tigger so much. They kept him in a small pen for most of the day. Though he had food and water, he didn't have much human or animal interaction. Obviously, that had something to do with his frightened reaction to new people.

Hearing the story turned our fear of Tigger into pity. Within about ten minutes, Tigger got used to us and eventually sat on Allyson's lap. It took him a little longer to warm up to me, but he did eventually. So in the end, we decided to buy Tigger and take him home. A purebred Yorkshire Terrier can easily cost around $1000. The Canes offered him to us for $300. But since Tigger obviously had baggage we were able to work them down to $200, which seemed fair to all of us. So we collected his things, carefully picked him up and headed out the door. At the doorway Groot and Katie gave Tigger one more goodbye rubdown. Katie began to tear up, but not Groot. I think he was happy to see Tigger go.

On the way home, Allyson proudly held our new doggie in her lap. He was about ten pounds of shaking and whining. Just about everything scared him. Occasionally he would break out into a mad barking fit, and we did our best to calm him down. We thought that if we could just get him settled at home things would go much better.

Before we got home, we realized that we needed some basic dog supplies: food and water bowls, dog food and treats, a kennel and a few toys. So we stopped by the store, where Allyson waited in the car with Tigger while I went in for supplies. About 20 minutes later I came back out to find Allyson trying to hush a panicked Tigger. She was flushed and had exhausted all of her sweet cute-doggy voice already.

She told me what set Tigger off: "I had the car window open a little so we could see out. A mom and her daughter passed by when Tigger went crazy! He was screeching and barking and tried to get out of the window to chase them down. They were both terrified and got away from the car. I tried to apologize, but they were already gone!" Tigger was calm at the moment, but Allyson was still pretty upset. She said, "Jason, I don't want to own a dog that people run from!"

I tried to stay supportive and optimistic about this dog that cost us $200 about an hour ago. He's not going back. No, we're committed to the little guy now. "Okay. Let's just get him home and I'm sure he'll settle down," I said, thinking that things couldn't get any worse.

And it did get a little better that night. He was timid in his new home and carefully sniffed around every room. I took him out of the house for a walk, which I thought he found delightful. But he wasn't very playful. I threw a toy some to try to get him to chase it while we walked in the field behind our apartment, but he wasn't interested in getting it. He seemed more concerned with scoping out his surroundings. That night we held him on the couch while we watched TV. He seemed suspicious of us but finally went to sleep on Allyson's lap. She and I gave each other a quiet high-five. Yes! Maybe he was finally learning to chill out!

At the end of the evening, we let him sleep on a pillow on the floor. Initially he whined a lot, and I could hear him quietly pace the bedroom floor from time to time, but eventually he went to sleep.

All God's creation has to go potty when they wake up. So the next morning I awoke, did my business, and took Tigger out to do his. He still seemed uncertain about Allyson and I, but we kept a kind tone in our voices. He liked the food we gave him for breakfast and we tried to give him a treat here and there to show him that we really were his friends. We thought he was coming along nicely and began to see Tigger as our own dog.

It was Saturday, and we wanted to show off the new addition to our family. So we invited Chuck and Amy over for dinner that night. They agreed to come over at six o'clock, so we designated a portion of the day for cleaning the house up and cooking dinner. While getting everything shipshape, I saw Tigger under the dining room table.

"What are you doing over there, buddy?" I said.

He ignored me and began walking circles around one spot he found particularly interesting. When I realized what he was really doing it was too late. He dropped and peed a sizable puddle right there.

And I reacted yelling "NO!" while I charged at him. When I reached him, his bladder was empty. I took him by the collar, stared him in the eye and said it again: "NO! Bad dog!"

Well, He didn't like that. Not one little bit. The tiny Tigger hunkered down and spread out his paws in a combat-like stance, all his fur pointed straight up. He bared his teeth, which I think grew out another inch, and let lose a hybrid snarl-growl of dark and supernatural proportions.

Tigger had become Cujo.

I almost made my own little puddle too before Allyson ran in to see the commotion. She thought the sound she heard was Tigger eating my leg. When she showed up I asked her to stay out of the room while I had it out with the devil dog. My voice stayed firm, but I softened up and slowed my movements. Eventually, Cujo left and we had Tigger again. We tried to get him comfortable before company arrived in the next few hours.

By six o'clock dinner was ready and the house was spick n' span. You could tell we made a big deal about the evening. Tigger seemed okay, too. We even put a handsome blue bow around his collar to make him look even nicer. Admittedly, it was a wimpy look, but we thought it might make him look a little more gentle...and a gentle evening was the goal. Chuck called me a little after six saying that they were running late but were just around the corner. Allyson and I looked everything over again as we hoped for a perfect evening. Tigger seemed nervous too, but then again, he was always nervous.

A simple knock at the door started all the commotion. Everything was a blur. Tigger charged the door amid a barrage of insane yelps. I tried to pull him back from the door, but he still must have held a grudge against me since he snarled at me too. Allyson tried to step in but Tigger growled and snipped at her. By the time I got between Allyson and the dog, Chuck and Amy opened the door and made their way inside.

The ten-pound Cujo charged them both. It only took a second for their sweet statements to change from "Hey there, little guy!" to a fearful "Holy Crap!" All of the commotion just fed Cujo's ferocity. In good faith, Amy bent down a little trying to pet the tiny wrecking ball only to meet growling, snapping, and snarling. Amy recoiled and screamed while Cujo repeatedly jumped up, biting at her hands. Chuck hopped in front of Amy, but Cujo kept coming.

I had already stumbled to my hands and knees watching the whole surreal event. At first I grabbed Cujo around the waist, but that was no good. He was like a little chainsaw roaring in all directions threatening to chew up whatever was in front of him. I had to contain this madness, so without thinking I treated the dog like a live grenade and jumped on top of him. I may have even muttered something like, "Save yourselves!" but I can't be sure. I was able to get my arms around the dog and my hand around his snout as he continued to spew muffled barks through his nose. For a few moments I scolded him while holding him stationary, then I remembered how well scolding worked earlier that day and changed my tactics.

"Please stop! Pretty please?"

After writhing on the floor with him for a few moments, Cujo refused to calm down. The only hope to salvage the evening was to isolate the dog, so I put him in the bedroom and closed the door. He was furious, barking incessantly and clawing at the door. He was so loud and obnoxious we could barely hear ourselves speak, but we tried to wait him out.

I came out of the bedroom with a half-untucked wrinkled shirt covered in dog fur, shaggy hair and tilted glasses smeared with dog saliva. I straightened my glasses, looked at everyone and said, "Well, who's hungry?"

Dinner was...awkward. We all were a little disheveled at the dinner table, and I'll bet you've already guessed the topic of the evening. We talked about Tigger and what we were going to do with him. During our conversation, the furry little chainsaw continued to hack away at the bedroom door. Everyone agreed that we just couldn't keep him. The whole conversation was uncomfortable, and nobody had much of an appetite. Even though we planned on watching a movie after dinner, Chuck and Amy decided to leave early.

Allyson and I felt terrible, but really who could blame our guests for leaving after all the commotion? We talked a little more about Tigger. The dog needed more than a new home; he needed rehabilitation or maybe an exorcist. In truth, we felt bad for him and knew he needed better care than we could give.

It was still early in the evening, so I called the Canes. And of course, Groot answered the phone. His deep voice boomed, "Hello?"

"Hi Mr. Cane, this is Jason Garrison. We bought your dog Tigger a few days ago."

"Yes, I remember. How's it going?"

"Actually, not good. We've tried everything we can to make it work, but he's attacked me, my wife, and tonight he tried to eat two of my friends. So you see, we just can't keep him."

There was a long silence. He finally responded, "Well, we're not prepared to take him back."

I winced and shook my head. Allyson could read my face. We thought this might happen, and had already talked through our options. I continued, "I wish that wasn't the case sir. We want to bring him back to his family. Otherwise, we'll have no other choice but to take him to a shelter. We'd really hate to do that. We'd prefer just to bring him back to you since you're his original family."

Again, there was a long silence and finally he exhaled. "I need to talk this over with my wife. Let me call you back," he said.

I agreed, hung up, and talked it over with Allyson. Since his outburst, Cujo had slowly become Tigger again, so we let him out of the bedroom. He made his displeasure clear by pooping and peeing on the floor. Under the circumstances, I just let it go. We had bigger problems at the moment. When he came out, he looked all over the house for the missing intruders, and he didn't seem too keen with us either. The feeling was mutual.

Within the hour, Katie called. She was apologetic about the whole ordeal and more than willing to take Tigger back. She said that she was worried about how things might go with us since the dog had some temperament problems. So instead of trying to find him a new home, they were willing to modify their schedules to make things work. That made Allyson and I feel a little better about the situation. So it was settled; tomorrow morning we'd take Tigger back home.

For the rest of the evening, we just let Tigger do as he pleased. We accepted that he was scared of us, and we of him. Oddly enough, I think we all wanted to make it work, too. Before the night was over, Tigger had jumped on the couch and fallen asleep on Allyson's lap again. It was bittersweet.

The next morning we hopped in the car and took Tigger back. He seemed a little more comfortable with us that day. We even questioned again whether or not we should return him, but we stuck to our guns. We really did want to keep Tigger, but ultimately we had to face the fact that we couldn't handle him. We thought his best bet for a happy life was with his original owners. Though the thought comforted us, it was a sad trip nonetheless.

When we pulled into the parking lot, Allyson agreed to stay in the car. She said, "So, you'll just give them the dog and they'll give you the check back, right?"

"Uh, yeah. That's the plan!"

Dang it, the $200! Honestly, I was mainly concerned about giving Tigger back. On the phone, I never even mentioned the money. I wish I had, because now I had to negotiate with the Incredible Hulk if he came to the door.

With Tigger in my arms I walked up the three flights of stairs wondering who would answer the door at the top. When I knocked on the door, it opened and I looked up at Groot.

Tigger yipped with joy and tried to jump out of my arms. Groot ducked through the doorway and took the happy dog with one giant mitt. I swallowed hard and thought *now I need to ask for the money.* Just then, Groot held out his left hand. Between two fingers was the check I wrote him days earlier.

"I'm sorry it didn't work out," he said. His expression didn't show much sympathy.

I took the check, "Believe me, we are too."

He nodded. Tigger was licking every part of Groot's hand. As Groot turned to go inside, I caught a glimpse of Tigger's tail. It was wagging.

WIENER DOGS ARE FAT

Allyson and I had mixed feelings on the way home at the end of that whole Tigger weekend. We were happy that we didn't have to take the dog to the pound and delighted that we got our money back, but the whole ordeal was pretty traumatic for us. We had hoped for a friendly dog that was happy to see us and ready to meet new people and other dogs. We wanted a wagging tail, not fur standing on end. We almost ended up with a dog that just seemed mad at the world.

We talked it over in the car ride home. "Why in the world did we even get that dog?" Allyson asked.

"I have no idea, babe. I think we were just so excited about the whole thing that we hoped everything would smooth over. I thought things would get better, but man that was way too much for us to handle!"

Allyson agreed: "When we first showed up and knocked on the door—do you remember?—Tigger sounded like he wanted to kill us!"

"Yeah, and when we took him home, he tried!"

We finally got a few minutes to laugh about the whole thing. Then I mused some more. "I think when I saw another Yorkie, I thought that it would be just like Scrabble. Even though he didn't act like her, I thought Tigger could be like her one day if we treated her just right."

"Maybe so," Allyson said. "I guess I was hoping for another B.J. too. All the Yorkies I know are sweet. I've never known one that charged after people like that."

"Yeah, I thought dogs of the same breed would act pretty much the same."

I could feel Allyson stare at me, but I just kept my eyes on the road. Allyson broke the pause, "Really?"

"Well, yeah! Sort of. I guess I thought we could make it work and everybody would be happy. Pie-in-the-sky kind of stuff. It's unrealistic isn't it?"

It was. Allyson and I concluded that we would have liked to help turn that dog around, but we didn't think we could do it. Plus, it would be our first dog together. We knew that taking care of a dog took responsibility, which we were prepared for, but this one required much more than that. Furthermore, we were still newlyweds growing accustomed to married life, which meant arguments over the toilet seat, toothpaste, socks left on the floor, and other really important things. Ironing these out would be tougher with a rabid dog stalking us from across the room.

We got home and breathed a sigh of relief. It was nice knowing that we didn't have to worry about the tiny banshee screaming at us as we walked in. And I was happy that I wouldn't have to wrestle a dog into submission. We made a few sandwiches for lunch and camped in front of the computer looking for other dog options. Since we had already tried to find a Yorkie, we figured that we'd give other breeds a try. We spend a few hours locked in research to determine which dog would be the perfect fit for us.

"What about a Beagle?" I said. "They are a little bigger than Yorkies, but not too big for what we're looking for. It looks like they are a good choice for families with kids, too. Once we decide to have kids, it would be perfect!"

"I like them too," Allyson said, "but it says here that they aren't a good choice for apartment complexes because they tend to howl a lot. Here, what about this: a Pug. It says they are great in apartments and good around kids."

"I'm not digging that smushed face and curly tail. They're cute and all, but it says here that they are considered toy dogs."

"What's the big deal about that?"

I shrugged. "Nothing, I guess. But I've seen those things run, and they look silly, like clowns running a footrace in floppy shoes. Let's just keep looking."

After a few more minutes searching the web, we saw a picture of a Bulldog.

"Aw yeah! I'm all over that one!" I said.

"I thought you said you didn't want a silly looking dog," Allyson said.

"Whatever! They may look dopy, but it says here that they are strong and fast. See, it says 'They are ideal for apartment complexes and don't need a great deal of exercise.' It's perfect!"

"Jay, those things are ugly. Look at these pictures. They've got slobber all over their faces. That stuff is gonna get all over our hands, and the furniture too!"

"Come on! The snot's pretty cool. It's manly!"

"No."

"*Humph!* All right, fine. What's next?"

"Umm…Jack Russell Terriers," she said.

I looked over the info on the screen. "This one looks great—small, friendly, energetic, and smart. Seems like it's what we're looking for."

"I know some people that have Jack Russells," Allyson said. "The dogs have so much energy, they need a lot of walking and exercise or they'll drive us crazy. I don't know that we can handle that while living in an apartment."

I agreed. After a few more minutes we came across another one of my favorites: a Basset Hound. They had a lovable face and friendly demeanor. But after reading the description I said, "I love these, but I'm afraid their long backs will make it hard for them to go up and down stairs."

Allyson said, "We'd have to carry them in that case to make sure they don't get hurt."

"Yeah, and it looks like they can get pretty heavy. Maybe we should wait on these until we get a house."

Taking note of another breed, I said, "Hey what about these: Cocker Spaniels."

"Those are great dogs," Allyson said. "I've known some families that had them over the years. They'd be a good choice. Except...."

"Except?"

"They get really excited a lot. And...well...they pee everywhere when that happens."

"Uh, huh. Next!"

Throughout the week we kept up our dog research and combed the ads in the papers for a suitable small dog. We were flying a little blind actually, since we still hadn't even decided which kind of dog we wanted. Allyson was more tenacious about the search than I was. Bogged down with uncertainty near the end of the week, she called her dad to get his opinion on which dog might be the best choice.

She told him the story about Tigger and confessed that we were now a little gun shy about getting any dog. That's when her dad suggested that we try to get a Dachshund. I heard her from the other room when she bleated out contempt, "Ew, no! We're not going to get some fat weenie dog!" I instantly envisioned the caricature of a ridiculously long dog with a voracious appetite. Its paws made enough contact with the ground to drag its bloated stomach from place to place. I smiled and thought, *At least that would make for shorter walks!*

When Allyson finished her phone call, we talked it over. She had thought that Dachshunds were lazy, since most of the ones that she had seen growing up were overweight. Her dad corrected her; it's not the lazy dog, it's the lazy human that won't take it for walks or play with it in the back yard. If we threw a ball with the dog just a few days a week and gave it a reasonable portion of food every day, it could stay nice and trim.

Allyson and I laughed as we took the notion more seriously. A *weenie dog!* We had never even considered it. Intrigued, we opened up the laptop again to investigate and read that Dachshunds weren't lazy at all. As scent hounds, they were bred to track and hunt badgers, rabbits, and prairie dogs. I even read that they could go underground into a badger's den to drive it out, which would take guts, especially since badgers were not exactly the friendliest of creatures. There's the fight I was looking for! We continued to read that they were loyal, happy, and curious dogs. The more we read, the more we liked them. Dachshunds only had one downside that we could pinpoint. Since they were unusually long, they were subject to back injuries. Likewise, climbing and descending stairs could be a problem. But we could simply carry the dog when we encountered stairs. He could walk everywhere else, no problem. So it was decided, and we started searching the newspapers for a Dachshund.

Turns out, there were many available in the Saturday paper, but none that we could afford. Most of the ads were from breeders who sold their dogs for top dollar, and we didn't have that kind of income. But we did find one that showed promise: DACHSHUND NEEDS NEW HOME! I called and got all of the info. The guy's name was Mark. He owned a red miniature Dachshund and had to find it a home fast since his landlord was upholding a no-dog policy. It was a purebred Dachshund about four-months old and very playful, and Mark was willing to let the dog go for an even $200, though he paid a lot more for it. What impressed me the most was how he kept emphasizing the fact that finding a good owner was more important than the money. I had a good feeling about this one, and it was such a great deal we asked if we could come out that afternoon to visit. We didn't want anyone else taking the dog out from under us. So we made the plans and showed up in the middle of the afternoon.

It was not an easy house to find. The directions took us out of the city into the middle of the country. We found the house, a bright garden home in the middle of a few green acres. Allyson gasped, "That would be the perfect home for a family with a dog. All that room to run and play! It's gorgeous!" We pulled up the long driveway and parked, both of us con-fessing our anxiety. Before we arrived, we agreed that we would need to scrutinize things a little better than last time. This dog would need to impress us or no deal.

Mark answered as soon as we knocked and invited us into his living room where we met two of his kids. His daughter was the oldest, about nine-years old, and his son was maybe seven. We introduced ourselves with big smiles, and they grinned back but we weren't entirely convinced that they were happy to see us.

Mark explained, "Yeah, they are not thrilled about today. You see when we moved here from California, I got them the dog to help make things easier. But the landlord won't let us keep him. He was really upset when he found out that we had a dog—I think he hates them. So, we've got to find him a new home one way or another."

Our hearts went out to the kids. They were only able to keep their new dog long enough to fall in love with him, and now these two strangers could be taking him away. I bet they thought that no one could love that dog more than they could; and really, it's tough to compete with the love of a family with kids. We sat on the couch and told them about ourselves, answering several of their questions. They asked us what we did for a living, what kinds of dogs we had owned before, where we were from, and other things. Later, we realized that they were interviewing us to make sure we were a good fit. When Allyson was talking, I noticed how nice the house looked. There were lots of windows that lit up the room on that sunny day. The living room was spotless, the walls painted with soft pastels. But I thought it was strange that we couldn't hear any barking since we showed up.

About ten minutes after our arrival, Mark looked at his kids and asked, "What do you think?" The smiles that they both had during our talk faded a little, but they both nodded. Mark then let us in on a secret. The kids wanted a say in who would get their dog, so the two oldest were a part of this initial conversation while the youngest played with the dog in the back bedroom. Now that we cleared the first round of screening, we got to see the dog.

The girl left to get him. After she walked down the hall, we heard a door open and the light galloping approached the living room. This was the moment of truth. A bright happy face emerged from the hallway. It was a red shorthaired weenie dog. His head was mere inches from the ground and he was about a foot long with a narrow tail that wagged incessantly. Clearly delighted to see us, he wore a panting smile on his face. His wide, floppy ears hung low until he saw us, then they perked up in curiosity. Dachshunds' ears don't go up as much as they go out; it's like watching the canvas on a sailboat catch wind. Those activated ears can double or even triple a dog's cuteness. They showed that he was curious and friendly. He looked at us like we were a part of his family that he had never met.

Allyson's heart melted, "Aw! What's his name?"

"Sparky!" one of the kids said.

Allyson looked at me with awe, "That is *perfect!*"

Well, Allyson's gone, I thought, but tried my best to hold on to skepticism. I wanted to make sure this was the right one for us. But our first impression of Sparky made it hard to find any faults. I found myself agreeing with Allyson, everything about Sparky seemed perfect so far. This was the kind of dog that we could have for the long haul. It's like he infected the whole room with cheer; everyone smiled and laughed when he showed up. He approached us immediately—that tail wagging so fast—and let us say hello. We stroked him and talked about how excited we were to meet him. We couldn't help ourselves; we had to get on the floor with him to play. He seemed to smile and then he vanished behind the couch only to emerge a moment later with a fluffy ball. He laid it down in front of me and gave me a look. Almost telepathically, I swear I heard him say, "Well?"

I picked up the half-mangled ball of fluff, which made him spin. "What do you want me to do with this?" I asked. He hunched down and gave a commanding bark. I tossed it behind the couch and—*Poof!*—he was gone in a flash, only to return and drop it in front of me again moments later.

"You're his friend for life now!" Mark said. The ball was Sparky's test of friendship. If you were kind enough to throw a toy for him, then you were all right. In fact, if you were a ball-tosser, Sparky thought you should never leave his side. Allyson and I took turns tossing while we got more info about Sparky. How much and how often did he eat? What kind of treats did they give him? Was he housebroken? How often did he go outside?

What we gathered was that Sparky was four-months old. He wasn't fully housebroken but was getting the hang of it. He went out at least three times a day and ate twice. We told Mark about our experience with Tigger and asked him up front if he had seen similar behaviors with Sparky. No, Sparky got in his moods like other dogs, but most of the time he was a very happy and energetic dog.

Things looked very good. It appeared all of my concerns had been quelled, and I started to think this was the dog for us. Playing with Sparky during the conversation made everybody happy. Everybody, that is, except Tommy. At about five-years old, he was the youngest of the three kids and played with Sparky in his bedroom when we first arrived, soaking up all the playtime he could get with the dog he was about to lose. He scowled at us the moment he came into the living room.

We made it clear that we were willing to take Sparky home, and I asked Mark again about price. He repeated the same number from earlier: $200. He also said that other people had called showing interest in Sparky though he was happy with us and would give him to us today for the price. We had great leverage for negotiation, and Mark knew it. The dog had to be gone by the end of the week, even if it meant the pound, and there was no guarantee that the other callers would work out or be willing to pay. I was pretty sure that I could work him down some.

Allyson and I stepped outside for a minute to talk it over, where she told me what I already knew: she wanted Sparky. We considered negotiating but the dog was too good to pass up. And a measly two hundred dollars for a purebred Dachshund puppy with a great disposition and raised by a loving family was a great deal. Anyway, it was fifty dollars cheaper than what we almost paid for Tigger last week.

We had just made our way back through the door when we heard the weeping. Mark and the older kids were trying to console a crying Tommy. He yelled, "IT'S NOT FAIR!" and sobbed again.

Mark pulled him close and said, "Tommy, we talked about this. Sparky can't stay with us."

"But he's *my* dog! He lives *here*!" Tommy cried. His brother and sister started to cry, too. They all embraced him and accepted the fact that Sparky was leaving today.

Allyson was so much better with kids than I was. She knelt down next to Tommy, put her hands on her knees and looked into his eyes. She said, "Tommy, I promise that we will take the very best care of Sparky. We will spoil him rotten! He makes us happy, and we will make him happy, too."

"Will you play with him?" he sniffed.

"Everyday!"

"Will you love him?"

"Forever and ever!"

His bottom lip trembled and stuck out. He nodded and whispered, "Okay."

Mark invited me to the kitchen table where I could write the check while the kids spent their last few minutes with Sparky. They had to call for him a few times to draw him out of hiding. All the commotion scared him back into the bedroom. He tiptoed his way into the den, hunched over with droopy ears. The kids took turns holding him, each of them trying to squeeze in a lifetime of hugs and strokes.

Mark approached the kids hesitantly; it was time for us to go. I followed Allyson's example and got on a knee next to the kids. "I'll take him when you're ready," I said softly. Sparky soaked up another minute of love until they handed him to me. His ears were still drooping, and he seemed concerned that everyone was sad. I took him in my arms and said, "Thank you so much for this. We will take good care of him." I got a little grin from them all.

As Allyson and I approached the door, Tommy ran up once more with tears in his eyes. I stooped down and he gently embraced Sparky's head with both hands. He slowly leaned forward until their heads touched, closed his eyes and whispered, "I love you, Sparky." He then turned around and hugged Mark, burying his head in his stomach.

As soon as we got into our car, Mark and his family went inside their home and closed the door. We pulled out of the driveway and started home. It was done. As we drove away, we noticed that Sparky was trembling all over. This whole ordeal was brand new territory for him. Allyson held him close and said, "Don't be scared, Sparky. We meant what we said. We really will love you forever!"

HE'LL LEARN IT ALL IN NO TIME

We noticed a couple of things in the car ride home. First, Sparky shook when he got nervous. He didn't tremble; he shook as if he was experiencing his own category-5 earthquake. If we were quiet for a few moments while it's happening, we could hear his jowls smacking as his long snout jerked left and right. The shaking also added an amusing vibrato to his whine. It started out pathetic and clear, then the shaking chopped the sorrowful whines into pithy chuckles. Allyson held him close to console him, and that's when we noticed something else. Sparky produced a ton of heat. An active dog, he must have had an incredible metabolism to make so much warmth. Allyson actually began to sweat as she held him. Sparky was warm to begin with, but all the spasms produced even more heat. He was panting, Allyson was sweating, and I hit the A/C feeling some pride in my new dog and some pleasure at the comical scene in the passenger seat. The fact that he could raise the temperature in the car by about ten degrees amid all his shaking earned him his first nickname: Volcano Dog.

It was getting dark when we got home; but before we went inside, I wanted to walk Sparky around the building so that he could take care of business. That way, we could introduce him to the sights and smells of his bathroom, which probably smelled like a community port-o-potty to him. So I went up to the apartment, got our leash, connected it, and we took him for a little walk. He was anxious to get out, and once his feet hit the ground he put his nose down and sleuthed around. It took him some time, but he finally peed, then we turned to go inside.

On the way, Allyson and I began to talk about picking him up to keep him from climbing the fifteen-foot staircase, but once he reached them he bounded up in seconds. Sparky was surprisingly nimble, and was ready to storm the second flight of steps if I hadn't stopped him. When we went inside, his nose hit the floor again. The apartment was a new place that he had to check out. I took him off his leash and he slowly walked around every room taking in all of the smells. That's when I first noticed the fur standing on end right where his back ended and his tail began.

I didn't know what to make of it. My mom owned a cat for several years and I was well-aware of what fur standing up on a cat meant, besides the fact that I would start sneezing within the next few minutes just because I was in the same room with it. Sparky didn't seem defensive, he was probably just nervous. These rooms were strange to him and much quieter since there were no kids around. The fur dropped a moment later until he caught a sent that really got his attention and the fur stood up again. Then it hit me. All the dogs and cats that lived in our apartment before probably left an interesting potpourri behind. It was why he kept checking all of the rooms. He could smell the other animals, even though they were nowhere to be found. Since Dachshunds are hounds, Sparky would probably notice them more than other breeds might, and I was sure it would take him some time to get used to them.

We gave him about an hour to explore, then tried to feed him. Shaking the food bag we sang out "who's hungry?" He was excited more about the theatrics and less about the food. It must have been his nerves that kept him from eating that night, but he sure did enjoy the water. Maybe the trembling had some role in his voracious thirst. Since he only ate a few kibbles of food, we decided to leave the bowl out for him while Allyson and I ate our own dinner. Of course, Sparky was much more interested in our cheeseburgers than his dry food. But though he whined and begged some, he stopped when we scolded him. I gave him a firm "NO." To which he put on his best penitent face, his ears drooped lower than I had ever seen, and he gave out a little grunt as he lay down.

It was impressive to see Sparky respond so well to our reprimand. He seemed quite familiar with the word *no*, which meant that his previous family might have spoiled him, but they also knew where to draw lines. We could tell that they loved him enough to show him gobs of attention and to show him what he was not allowed to do. That made our job all the easier.

We were also happy that Sparky proved he'd had some potty training, and I did my best to follow through and reinforce what he knew. After dinner, Sparky followed me into the kitchen where I put up the dishes. I then turned to him and said with the biggest smile and enthusiasm I could muster, "You wanna go outside?" I mentioned earlier that all Dachshunds' ears go outward; but when they are intrigued, they went nearly vertical while the floppy ends nearly cover their eyes. Sparky's eyes were opened in excitement, his ears hovering just above his brow. All four legs on the ground, he stood as tall as he could, towering at maybe ten inches. His tail wagged at an uncertain rhythm. *Am I supposed to be happy and excited right now?*

I grabbed a bright blue plastic poop bag, a few treats, and his leash and walked to the front door. Sparky ran there too and began to bark out his excitement. I hooked his leash, and opened the door. He ran to the edge of the stairs and stopped, looming down the flight. He darted from side to side, trying to find a way down. Obviously, coming up was no problem for him, but going down would be a challenge. But he figured he'd try it anyway. His two front paws hopped down the first step and he froze when he realized there was no room for his rear. I held his leash taut so he couldn't tumble and just watched. He finally got his two hind legs down on the same step, but he decided that was as far as he wanted to go. It took about twenty seconds to descend one stair with fear and trembling—not very efficient. Finally, I scooped him up in my right arm and took him down to the first floor.

He finally relieved himself after walking around on the grass a few minutes, and I treated him like he just won the AKC Best in Show, praising him, stroking him, and feeding him a liver treat. He was thrilled. But after about ten more minutes of walking around, he didn't poop. So we finally went back inside where Allyson also congratulated Sparky on a job well done. We figured the stress kept him form eating, which meant no poop tonight. As long as I didn't find any surprise chocolate clumps on the floor that night, I'd stay happy.

Sparky wanted to celebrate his urinary victory by playing. While we cheered, he grabbed the first toy he could find. It was a fluffy lamb squeaker-toy the size of an orange. He snagged it and gave us a playful growl while romping around the room, daring us to take it from him. We chased and threw and dragged that toy all over the living room. Sparky could have played until morning, but he eventually wore us out. He finally took the hint that we were finished when we moved from the floor to the couch. After running around the living room a few times emitting playful growls and occasionally shaking the toy in furious joy, he jumped up on the couch between us. He kept the slobbery toy in his paws and gnawed on it quietly until the squeaks grew weaker and he dozed off. That lamb became his favorite toy, and somehow it got the name Babies.

Around eleven o'clock it was bedtime, and we had already made arrangements for our new perfect dog. I prepared a special pillow and blanket laid next to my side of the bed. We'd close the bedroom door and keep the lights off. I thought he'd like it fine. So I took him outside once more and then went into the bedroom, again making a really big deal about his bed. It was the best, most fantastic cushion any dog could hope for. What more could a dog need? I placed him and his Babies on the cushion, praised him and slipped into bed. When I turned off the lights, I thought all was well with the world. We now have the perfect dog.

Ally and I just got comfortable when we heard the whining. It began as a low and even polite whimper to see if anyone would respond. Within minutes, it grew into steady whines that mimicked the sounds he made in the car. Though it was pitch black, he was obviously shaking since the whines ended with pathetic chuckles.

"It's okay, Sparky. We're here! Just lay down and go to sleep," said Allyson. We both tried to console him, to let him know that he wasn't alone in this strange new home. But it just made things worse. Now that he knew our location, he began clawing at the side trying to get into the bed with us.

"He's used to sleeping with those kids," I said. "We've got to try to wait him out." We thought it was a good plan, but not Sparky. His clawing on the mattress became frantic. He tried to climb each side, his whining progressing into an ear-piercing screech. We heard him pant and gasp wildly as he moved from side to side hoping to find some way to get to us. Twenty minutes passed in what seemed to be an hour while Sparky continued his tantrum. His screams had become agonizing howls.

I don't know who caved first. I think it was Allyson. "What are we going to do?" she asked. "The neighbors are going to have us evicted!" I was worried about that, too. We could normally hear people walk upstairs and could sometimes hear the television on downstairs. Those are the kinds of things you get used to in an apartment. They are things you expect. But Sparky's howls at midnight? That was too much. Not to mention the sounds they must have heard last week when we hosted Tigger the killer Yorkie. They might wonder if we have some kind of dog-fighting getup.

So we finally agreed to let him come up into our full-sized bed just for the night. We didn't want to make a regular thing out of it, but we thought that he might be especially nervous about things because he'd only been home with us for a few hours. But I was sure he would adjust in no time. *Just for tonight,* I thought. Allyson leaned over and retrieved Sparky from the floor. He licked us both in gratitude, burrowed under the sheets between us, and quickly fell asleep.

Around six the next morning sunlight began to creep through our shades and Sparky decided it was time for us to wake up. My head was in the pillow when he stuck his long snout under my face and began licking my nose. I pushed him back and rolled over, trying to catch a few more winks. He tried licking my mouth next. "Stop it!" I said and pushed him back again. A few minutes later, he lay down next to my head and stared at me. I felt his snout breathing over my eyelashes. When I opened my eyes, I saw his nostrils but I just tried to ignore him. So he changed his strategy and laid his head down on top of my nose and mouth. I suppose he thought, *Since you're too lazy to get up, let's see if you're too lazy to breathe.*

I pushed him off my face and tried to get some more sleep. In my stupor, I heard him stir around on the bed and then I heard a thump on the floor. He'd jumped down. That's when I stretched and thought about sleeping for another hour or so, even though I was sure I could use a trip to the bathroom. My eyes popped open. *Sparky has to go to potty!* I shot up out of bed and said with a happy voice, "You wanna go outside?" Sparky appeared out of nowhere and began to hop.

All the sudden action jerked Allyson awake: "What's going on?"

"Sparky's got to go outside!" I said in the best celebratory voice I could muster at the crack of dawn. "I'll take him out!"

I was on a mission. I got dressed and took Sparky out quick as a flash. As soon as we made it to the grass, he dropped down to release a nice, long stream of relief—I was envious. "Good boy!" I said while my knees began to draw together. I had hoped that he would go poo now since he didn't the previous night. I kept him out a long as I could, but he seemed more interested in exploring than pooping. I couldn't hold it any longer, so we came back inside so I could make my own pit stop.

Allyson was up when we came in and eager to feed Sparky. He seemed more comfortable with us that morning and was definitely ready to eat more than a few kibbles. He did a few spins when Allyson poured out the food into his dish. It only took about a minute for him to finish and lap up his fair share of water. After that, we played with him on the floor again, not able to get past how great this new dog was.

Since it was Sunday morning, Allyson and I began to get ready for church, which left Sparky to his lonesome. He was gnawing on his Babies in the living room while we showered, shaved and dressed. He came looking for us once he realized that he was alone. It became clear that he didn't want to be left alone. But even when he was in the bedroom with us, he would occasionally wander the apartment. We didn't give it a second thought. He probably had things to do like exploring some more nooks and crannies, getting some water, or finding a new toy. When we walked past the kitchen we found a petite mound of dog poo under the dining table.

My tone with Sparky had been pleasant high notes since we met him, but upon seeing his little deposit, I dropped it to an authoritative bass. "Sparky, come here."

His trembling ear emerged around the corner first. Once he crept into full view, I could see that his whole posture was an apology. His ears looked like they were melting downward and his head was virtually dragging on the floor. His back was arched and his tail tucked. Allyson saw him come in and showed sympathy, something that his look evoked in me, too; but we had to address the tiny, smelly elephant in the room if we wanted Sparky to be fully housebroken.

I cupped my hand under his barrel chest and pulled him closer to the scene of the crime, scolding him with a lot of finger shaking. Volcano Dog shook and radiated heat. What I knew about housebreaking was limited, but I did know that you had to teach the dog that a potty in the house leads to discomfort while a potty outside should feel like winning a sweepstakes. During our scolding, he growled a little and the fur on his rear began to rise. I expected that and took that as a good sign. This dog had some spine after all! He wanted to please us but wasn't a pushover. That was something that made the housebreaking a little easer.

When it was done, I cleaned up the mess and made sure to play with Sparky a few minutes so that we could let bygones be bygones. Allyson spent a few minutes with him too until it was time to go. As we walked to the front door and closed it behind us, we could hear him whine and begin to bark. He was loud. We even heard him while we waited in the parking lot. We could have simply driven away, but we wanted to know about how long it would take him to stop. About 15 minutes passed until he started to ease up, and calmed down completely a few minutes later. Relieved, we drove to church. Being gone for about two hours would be a good test for him, we thought.

"I'm glad he's quiet now," Allyson said, "but there's no way we can let him roam the house while we're gone all the time. We'll have to figure out where he will stay when we aren't in the house."

GROOMING IS A BREEZE

When we left church, Allyson and I went shopping for a baby gate. Allyson was right, we didn't want a dog that was barely housebroken to roam the apartment all day while we were gone. Her work schedule was different from mine, so most days Sparky wouldn't be left alone for too long. Still, we decided pinning him up in the kitchen would give him plenty of room and access to his water bowl during the day. The kitchen we had was nothing special, but it had an open space with a window looking into the living room, which wouldn't give Sparky a claustrophobic feeling. The linoleum floor certainly was preferable over the carpet if he decided to relieve himself. A baby gate would block the kitchen's entrance perfectly without obstructing his view. This would also solve our problem of his sleeping in our bed. We would make him a nice cushion in the kitchen next to his food and water dishes—we were confident it would become his favorite place.

When we got home, just putting the key in the deadlock set Sparky off barking. "Yeah! We've got ourselves a guard dog!" I said.

"Sure," Allyson said. "Beware of the eight pound weenie dog on the other side. Mind your shins!"

I opened up the door where we saw the little hot dog, bright eyed and tail wagging at first sight. "Well a burglar won't know that," I said. "Besides, the fact that he'd make such a racket when he heard someone would at least be a deterrent, don't you think?" Just then Sparky approached and dropped his Babies at my feet. I gave the stuffed lamb a toss and he scurried after it.

"I guess," Allyson said with a chuckle. Then she looked around the whole apartment to see if Sparky left us any presents. I joined her in the search, but neither one of us could find any wet spots. We both took him for a walk right after that. Sparky already was learning what our phrases meant. "You wanna go outside?" was quickly becoming one of his favorites.

Sparky relished in the walk, enjoying it so much that going potty seemed to be the last thing on his mind. We were ready to go in but Sparky still hadn't produced anything. We took him to the grass and tried to reason with him, telling him "Go poop!" and "Go pee!" He just looked at us with half-wilted ears. He wasn't getting it. It wasn't until he finally squatted to pee that we celebrated and fed him his treat, a soft liver cube that we tried to convince him was the best tasting morsel in the world. He seemed to be getting it now. Pee out here: good. Pee inside: bad.

We were very proud of Sparky. The more time I spent with him, the more my old feelings that small dogs were wimpy began to ebb away. I noticed on the walks that everyone who saw us with our weenie dog always made cheerful efforts to say hello. I thought people would make fun, but they actually thought Sparky was the coolest...and he really was. He didn't have a pink bow or anything that accentuated cuteness; he was naturally cute without dainty effects. When he walked around, he held his head up high—nearly ten full inches off the ground—his barrel chest sticking out. Our new dog was awesome, and I thought it was time the Farmers knew, too.

Allyson agreed; it was time for round two with Chuck and Amy. I called and invited them to dinner at our house again. Chuck was hesitant, but I assured him we got the dog thing right this time. We wouldn't do a movie, just dinner and we could see how the night played out after that. He checked with Amy, who seemed a little reluctant, but since they didn't have any dinner plans already, they agreed to show that evening.

A special meal might help things go well, we thought, so we decided to prepare spaghetti with meatballs and a salad. But before we started dinner, we devoted some of the afternoon to a nap, then cleaned up a little and decided to do our best to make Sparky look nice. Unfortunately for him, that meant we were giving him a bath.

We placed all we needed in the bathroom and got organized: anti-flea shampoo, a water pitcher for rinsing, a few towels on the floor for drying, and we even had a little brush. Now that we were prepared, we started the water running in our tub and called for Sparky. Our one-bedroom apartment was humble and our bathroom was small. I'd never really thought of it before, but the sound of the tub filling in such a small bathroom can be atrocious. The tiled walls and linoleum floor only amplified the sound of the faucet crashing gobs of water into the metal tub. For the first time, I wondered what a small dog like Sparky would make of it. Where was he anyway?

The tub now had enough water, so I turned if off and called for Sparky again. Allyson called too, then giggled, "There is no way he's coming in here will-ingly!"

"No, I guess not," I said with a grin. "We'd better go get him."

We covered the whole apartment, but no Sparky. He wasn't in the living room, dining room, kitchen, or bedroom. I thought he might be hiding under one of the cushions that lined the back of our couch, but when I pulled them off, he wasn't there. Allyson went through the blankets that we used for our nap, but he wasn't there either. We even checked the pantry and walk-in closets on the ludicrous chance he had gotten closed in one of them. But still no dog. We were actually getting nervous, wondering if he was even in the house. But how in the world could he not be?

"Found him!" Allyson called. "He's in here!"

I walked into the bedroom and found Allyson flat on the floor, her head turned sideways speaking sweetly to something under the bed. She was trying to coax Sparky to come out, but he wasn't moving. The full-sized bed was old and heavy, something Allyson had since she was a teenager. There wasn't a great deal of room underneath it, but it was roomy enough for Sparky's new hideout. Allyson reached her arm under the bed as far as it would go, just up to her shoulder. "He's right in the middle of the bed. I can't reach him," she said, her voice muffled under the mattress. She seemed amused and agitated all at the same time.

"Keep reaching! Let me get on the other side and see if I can flush him out," I said. I got flat on my stomach and looked underneath but couldn't see anything. A few moments later, my eyes adjusted and I saw Sparky's silhouette, hunched over with wilted ears. I called out to him. His eyes glistened when he looked at me, but he would not be moved. I put my arm underneath and was just able to graze his side, but he simply slid over half an inch to get out of my reach. As Allyson and I strained to touch him, our best and sweetest calls in muffled tones, he waited patiently and comfortably in the center of the bed. Frustrated, I repositioned myself and pushed my arm in even further this time, brushing my fingertips on his ribs once again. He glanced at me calmly then slowly crept to the head of the bed, which was flush against the wall and flanked by our two heavy nightstands. Checkmate. My red face wedged under the oak frame, I look across at Allyson's face and made an observation: "I think he's done this before."

Sure he had. His former family had certainly bathed him more than once. The unmistakable roar of the filling tub coupled with our sudden interest in him seemed to make that clear. We had never bathed him, but he knew what the signs meant; and now he'd found the perfect spot to camp when we needed him. We thought about waiting him out but didn't have the time. The Farmers were coming over soon and he needed a bath. Allyson and I talked it over with our heads still fastened under the bed frame. Consequently, Sparky was pleased enough to lay his head down and attempt a nap—the little jerk.

"Let's coax him out with a treat," Allyson said. She left the room and came back with a small bag of liver cubes. At first she put a cube just beyond the bed so that Sparky could see it and then called him. No dice. The dog was unfazed. "Maybe if he smelled it…" she said lying down on the floor once again. Treat in hand, she reached underneath calling in a syrupy voice, "Here Sparky! Look at what I got for you! Your favorite!" It was hard for him to resist as Allyson gently squished the moist treat between her fingers. He crept forward and took the treat before Allyson could grab his collar. After he saw what she was trying, he had no interest in coming any closer even for liver cubes.

"I have an idea" I said, wiggled my head out of bondage, and left the room. Allyson peeked around the bed, only to see me emerge with our broom and a wicked little smirk. "We'll give you one more chance Sparky!" I said, a little too proud of myself. "Come out with your hands up or we'll have to send in a sweeper!" I had obviously seen way too many movies.

Of course, nothing happened. But once I put the broom under there and began sweeping toward him, a furry red lightning bolt shot out of the room. We walked out and found Sparky on the couch in a distressed posture: hunched over, tail tucked, ears wilting, and fur standing halfway up his back. I never imagined that it would petrify him like that, but since then he has never been fond of the broom.

The bathwater had gotten cold, so we drained it and started the faucet again. The roaring water made Sparky's fur stand on end. Allyson held him as we walked in the bathroom, and once he saw the water he climbed her like a tree, ending up almost completely on her shoulders. I peeled him off her as if he were a cat and placed him in the warm water. It wasn't deep, just barely touching his chest. He gawked at the water and tried pulling his paws out one at a time. He seemed more sickened by the water than afraid of it, and lathering him up just made it worse. After trying to jump out a few times, he finally succumbed to the process.

We took him out—celebrating, of course—and dried him off with towels and a hair-drier on a low setting. He complained the whole time, jerking, growling, and barking out his displeasure. He even attacked the hair drier like it was some sort of mechanical monster. When we turned him loose, he ran loops around the apartment, rolling on the carpet to get that icky bath water off. But we weren't finished with him yet.

We sat down on the living room floor and played with him and his Babies for a few minutes and then rolled out the rest of our tools: a towel, a brush, cotton balls, rubbing alcohol, and dog nail clippers. The towel created a workplace on the floor where we could brush Sparky's fur out. His fur was short and thin making it almost unnecessary. Then Allyson cleaned out his ears with an alcohol soaked cotton ball. We learned that Dachshunds have floppy ears that can get dirty and infected easily, so we wanted to keep them clean. Sparky didn't mind either task. So I nonchalantly put him in my lap, picked up the clippers and carefully aimed for his left-front paw.

Sparky's tail stopped moving, as did the rest of his body. His eyes were fixed on the clippers. When I moved them closer he let out a slow growl and his ears went way up over his eyes, another warning to cease and desist. "Now, now, Sparky. I've got to do this," I said as I held one of his toes and gently snipped the first nail. He growled and bore his teeth, probably more scared than angry.

After the first clip he wouldn't let me cut any more nails. Each time the clippers drew near a nail, he would jerk his paw back and nip at them. To his credit, he was careful to attack the clippers and not me. Allyson had to help me hold him, but even she wasn't enough to keep him from wildly squirming his paws loose just before each clip. Eventually we devised a plan and covered the top of his head loosely with a rag so he couldn't see what I was doing. It worked great. He froze until he heard the *snip!* and then growled out his worst obscenities.

Everything was moving along well until he went wild after a snip. It sent him into a fit with screams and yelps for help. We removed the rag on his head and he climbed up to Allyson's shoulder again. We eyed that nail now oozing blood; I had cut it to the quick. We both apologized and Allyson coddled him for a few minutes, her eyes were moist. "Don't do that again!" she said. "I don't think I can hold him with you if that keeps happening. I can't take him screaming like that."

"I'll do my best. Let's try to finish up," I said. We both knew that drawing blood would happen sometimes, and the fact that I was new at clipping nails meant that it would happen more rather than less. So she reluctantly agreed to help and though Sparky put up more of a fight this time, we got through it with no more blood. Of course, we celebrated.

LOSING THOSE IS NOT A GOOD IDEA

Once we heard the knock, Sparky sounded the alarm and barked his way to the front door. Chuck came in first, probably running reconnaissance for Amy who was a few steps behind him. But Chuck's response to Sparky signaled the all-clear for her to enter, too.

"You must be Sparky!" he said and stooped down to give him a friendly rub. Sparky's tail wagged faster and accepted all the attention he could get. "Oh my goodness! He's so cute!" Amy said and got on her knees to say hello. Sparky took all the strokes and scratches then galloped away, returning with a plush lamb in his mouth. He laid it in front of them and started to bark. When Chuck tossed it, Sparky returned it like clockwork and the friendship ceremony was complete. Allyson and I looked at each other and grinned. Sparky was a winner.

We sat down in the living room for a while, where Sparky had decided to sit in Chuck's lap and chew contently on his Babies. "He's so warm!" Chuck said.

"Yeah, we can't get over that," I said. "He's so high strung, he must have a really fast metabolism. Lucky for him he's got such short fur. Any thicker and he'd get too hot."

"He'll be good to have on the couch with you in the winter. That's for sure," Amy said.

"Or in the bed," Allyson added. "I imagine he'd be better than an electric blanket. When my sister and I were growing up, we let our dogs sleep in bed with us. But Jason doesn't want to do that."

I chimed in. "I'm just sayin' we'd all be happier with our own space. It's already cramped with both of us in that full-sized bed without a dog. I'll probably end up rolling on top of him or something. And if he gets fleas, we're gonna get eaten alive!"

"Yeah," Chuck said, "We'd rather keep Scrabble in her kennel at night. She loves it. She used to prefer the bed. But we kennel trained her since she was a puppy, and now she'd rather sleep there."

"Not all the time," Amy said. "She gets to sleep with us from time to time."

"She doesn't get in the way?" I asked.

"No, you get used to it, and when we move around she gets out of the way," Chuck said. "But mostly she stays in her kennel."

"Well last night we tried making him a spot on the floor, but he pitched a fit until he got his way," I said. "The kids who had him before us let him sleep in bed with them."

"That'll be an uphill battle," Chuck added, "since the kids let him do that for so long. If he's used to that, that's what he'll expect. You'll have to stick to your guns."

"We have a plan now," I said nodding to the baby gate leaning against the wall. "We'll make him a nice bed in the kitchen and pin him up in there. He'll get used to it."

"A kennel might be a better option," he said, "but I hope that works out. Remember that you gotta be re-

JASON GARRISON

solved. He'll do everything he can to make you do what he wants."

We talked a little more and then moved to the dinner table. Sparky was pretty good in that venue, too. He did some begging, but when we told him *no*, he got the message and lay down at our feet. About that time, Chuck said something pretty ballsy.

"Are you going to get him neutered?"

I was about to take a bite of a meatball, but took a sip of tea instead. "Well, I...I guess so," I muttered. "Ally and I haven't really talked about it yet."

"Sure we will," Allyson said. "We're not planning on breeding him and he'll definitely be easier to handle that way." She stabbed a meatball with a fork and cut it in half, sopping up a generous amount of marinara before eating it.

I drank more tea.

"You may want to do it pretty soon," Chuck said. "If you do it early enough, you'll catch him before he learns to lift his leg."

"Whoa, wait. You mean while he's a puppy?" I asked. This was new territory for me. I knew all about neutering and spaying but never had to decide when to do it to one of my own dogs. The talk about neutering a puppy like Sparky sounded as outrageous to me as sterilizing a ten-year old boy. *Let the dog live a little* I thought. "Isn't it too soon to do something like that?"

"Actually, it's probably perfect timing," Allyson said. "Growing up, we had our dogs neutered and spayed as early as we could."

"Why do that so early?" I asked. "Why not let him, you know, enjoy those things for a while?"

"Lots of reasons," said Chuck. "Eventually, he'll want to start marking his territory, and he'll mark the walls, furniture and drapes—really, everything. He'll even get more aggressive. He'll try to get away from you a little more so that he can, you know, sow his oats. Unless you want to breed him, neutering him early is the best way to go."

"It's true for the females too," Amy said. "We had Scrabble spayed as soon as we could. If not, she would start her period and we'd have to worry about putting a diaper on her once a month."

"Yeah," Chuck said and looked at me. "You remember how I had to do that for Molly? A few times the diaper would come off and I'd have to clean everything up. There was blood all over the place. Man, that was awful!"

Yeah, thanks Chuck. I had tried to forget that. Chuck didn't spay Molly because he thought about breeding her. More than once I recall his scrubbing the whole house down when that diaper came off. Maybe Molly wasn't as low-maintenance as I thought. All the memories came back to me as I stared into my marinara-covered noodles. I gulped down more tea, looked at Allyson and said, "Well, I guess that's something we'll have to look into tomorrow." Glancing down I noticed Sparky staring at me, trembling. "Look at him! He's already petrified!"

"No," Amy laughed, "He just wants a meatball!"

Chuck took a bite of garlic bread. "I'll bet he wants two."

****

The evening was a success. The Farmers enjoyed meeting Sparky and it looked like the feeling was mutual even though they recommended his castration. Sparky barked them to the door on their way out. Allyson and I came to realize that when Sparky accepted someone into his home, he would never grant him or her the right to leave. Once the Farmers closed the door, he stopped the yipping and looked at both of us—tail wagging—verifying that we were still in his life. He even brought his Babies to us for good measure, that symbol of his friendship. If we're playing with him, we weren't going anywhere. And, of course, who could say no to such a great dog?

"Who wants to go outside?" Once I said it, Sparky darted back and forth and gave a single bark. He was learning our phrases and commands quickly. I took him out where he spent most of his time exploring and sniffing, but my reminders to "go pee!" and "go poo!" finally paid off. And, of course, we had a small party after each movement. I'm sure the sleeping neighbors were just as impressed.

Once we came inside, the moment of truth had arrived: bedtime. We had a keen strategy for the evening. I set up the gate at the kitchen entrance, made a makeshift bed for Sparky on the linoleum floor and lay there with him for a little while until he started to fall asleep. It was going well, but any time we moved, he sensed it and hopped up. We weren't going to leave as easily as the Farmers did.

After a little while, Allyson went on to bed and I stuck it out for another few minutes. Once he fell asleep I started to sneak out, but he picked up on my slightest moves. I felt like an elephant trying to hide behind a sapling when he glanced at me, his ears raised asking "Where you goin'?"

"Go to sleep, buddy," I whispered. "We'll see you in the morning." Then I stepped over the gate, closed the bedroom door and slipped into bed.

"You think he bought it?" Allyson whispered. Just then, the whining began. Sparky couldn't bear the thought of being alone.

"I guess not," I grumbled.

But we stuck it out. The whines became barks. *Don't listen!* I thought. The barks became howls. *We gotta stick this out!* Then the howls intertwined with barks, whines, groans, whoops, chatters, gargles, hyperventilation, scampering, clawing, and…was that a cat screeching? We were surprised that such a small dog could produce so much noise. And it didn't sound like he was merely upset, it sounded like he was being murdered. Or maybe I was just thinking of what the neighbors wanted to do to me. Amid all the bellowing coming from our eight-pound dog, I tried reasoning with myself. People who live in apartments should expect to hear noises like this every now and then. *They can tolerate this for a little while.* Then I heard the gargling again and thought *But this sounds like we're conducting an exorcism!*

I was tired when it finally happened, so I can't remember who caved first. It must have been Allyson. We let Sparky out and let him sleep with us again that night. We thought that he might need just a few more nights to get used to the new home. Just before I fell asleep, I thought I heard something. But it was probably just my ears still ringing from all the commotion.

To the best of my recollection, it sounded like a single word.

"Sucker."

★★★★

The next day, Allyson was more obsessed with balls than Sparky was, searching the Internet for all the information she could about neutering dogs. All the info she found verified what we learned the night before. Sparky was old enough to have the procedure. It could be done in a few hours and he'd be back to normal in the next day or two.

Back to normal. That didn't sound right. But I went along with it. I had to confess that I liked Sparky the way he was. Once he was old enough for the testosterone to start flowing, they say he'd change—marking his territory and becoming prone to aggression. We weren't okay with that, so Allyson called several of the vets in the area to price out the procedure, and ultimately found a non-prophet organization that was the least expensive option. She checked out their credentials finding them highly qualified and set up the appointment.

Sparky was bright-eyed and happy when we dropped him off before we had to go to work. Allyson and I met at home at the end of the day and went to get him together. When they brought him out, he was happy but stoned: his eyes glassy, ears drooping, tail wagging a lot slower than we were used to seeing. We paid the bill and they gave the stoner dog to Allyson. At first he crawled into her arms, shaking, and stared her down with his worried, watery eyes. His look said something like, "They touched me in my private spot!"

Allyson giggled incessantly, holding him close while I checked under the hood. Sure enough, a dainty flap of skin sewed up with several stitches was all that remained of his manly package. Our beans and weenie dog was now just a weenie dog.

When we got in the car, Allyson gave him his Babies to cheer him up, but he wasn't interested in chewing on the little lamb. Apparently babies were the last things on his mind.

THEY SHARE AND SHARE ALIKE

That first five months Sparky was in our lives, lots of things changed. On the plus side, he had nearly perfected his potty training. Anytime we took him out he knew exactly what to do, but sometimes it took a little bit of time for him to do it. He had to sniff around and enjoy the outdoors a while unless he really had to go, in which case he would relieve himself as soon as he reached the grass. Once he got the hang of it, his bladder control was impeccable. If we took Sparky out and were in a hurry to get back in, he could void on command. Say "Go pee!" and he would drop. "Go poo!" would start him sniffing around furiously. He would then make a circle like an airplane preparing to land, lower his rear landing gear and drop his smelly cargo. Then he performed his post-poop dance, clawing at the ground as if to cover his steaming present. Sparky had turned bowel movements into interpretive movements.

He learned things so quickly, we taught him some tricks just to help him show off to our friends. After just a few days of work, Sparky could sit, shake, speak, lie down and roll over. The grand finale of his tricks was "being a bear," in which case he would sit straight up like a thirteen-inch column, balancing his whole body on his rear. It was amazing what he would do for a few soft liver treats.

Even though we had fun, there were also a few scares along the way. Allyson called me at work one afternoon saying, "I think I yanked Sparky's teeth out!" She had been on the floor with him playing with his Babies having a great time until she noticed blood and teeth on the toy. "Should I call the vet?" she asked.

"No, I'm sure it's fine. I wonder if it's his puppy teeth falling out," I said, glancing down at the scratches those little needles had left on my arms when I played with him a few days earlier. She decided to give the vet a call just in case and called me back a few minutes later. A little embarrassed, she said the vet confirmed that it probably was just his puppy teeth falling out. As any supportive husband would do, I suggested that only a dog abuser would yank a puppy's teeth out. I could hear her smile on the other end as she replied, "Shut up."

We also did our best to socialize Sparky. He did well around people, but we were also concerned about getting him around other dogs. He saw dogs here and there around the neighborhood when we went out for walks, but we wanted to introduce him to more than that, showing him a variety so that he'd be comfortable around them all. Well, we wanted him to feel at ease around *most* of them. A small dog always needs to be wary around bigger, more aggressive company. Luckily, dog parks were becoming popular around the Dallas area, and a new one had opened up nearby. So we picked up the leash, poop-bags, and a tennis ball, the latter earning Sparky's undivided attention, and said, "You wanna go for a ride?" He sure came to love that phrase!

We had a travel kennel that we'd put Sparky in when driving to the vet or on long drives, but usually we let him ride in our laps for short trips. He lived for rides like this one, darting around from window to window to take in all of the new sights. Once we arrived at the dog park, we leashed him up and led him to the entry gate. There were two fenced areas to choose from: one for small dogs and one for large ones. It was clear that the best fit for Sparky was the small-dog area, though no one was in there at the time. Still, it gave him plenty of room to get used to the environment, including the sights, sounds, and smells of the other pack of dogs playing in the neighboring section just a stone's throw away.

The first few minutes he sniffed around to get familiar with the new turf. I'm sure it was a complex bouquet of scents twice as potent as the ground around our apartment. The fact that the fur had risen halfway up his back indicated that he was intrigued and maybe nervous. He was busy sniffing until we pulled out the tennis ball, which made him forget the world around him completely. The drill was pretty simple, but so much fun. Throw ball. Sparky brings it back and lays it at my feet. Pick it up. Repeat.

We'd do our best to come up with some variety on the procedure. Pretend to throw the ball and hide it instead, making Sparky run frantically all over trying to find it. For more fun we'd keep pointing away saying, "go get it!" with an urgency that drove him to look even harder. Then I'd hold the ball up high until he saw it. He seemed surprised every time: *Where'd you get that?* Another fun idea was to sit on the ground and hide the ball under a leg or in a pocket. He'd soon sniff it out and try to dig it free. That was fun until he clawed my leg raw.

One thing was certain, Sparky was the fastest wiener dog I had ever seen. The way he bolted after the tossed ball got a fair amount of attention from the people in the large dog area, and some of them struck up a conversation with us. After a while, we noticed that we were still the only ones in the small-dog area and a number of people had dogs the same size as Sparky on the other side. We decided it was time for Sparky to put on his big-boy pants and move over to the big dog world.

Everyone was pleasant when we walked in, and Sparky didn't even realize that we made the transition into the world of large dogs since he was still fixated on his ball. We wanted him to strut a little bit more, so we showed off all of his tricks. But none of these were as impressive as Sparky's outright speed. Soon, a few people wanted to throw the ball for him, and Sparky didn't discriminate; anyone willing to give it a toss made the occasion all the happier for everyone. One of the things that made people laugh the most was how little Sparky could fit a whole tennis ball in his mouth. He had to open as wide as possible and wedge the thing in there each time, and he took such great delight in it.

Sparky preferred the long throws all the way across the dog park so he could sprint as fast as possible. Now, a tennis ball thrown across a field like that piqued the interests of lots of other dogs, and that was something Sparky didn't know how to manage yet. One of the tosses roused a mutt that looked like a mid-sized Doberman Pincher. Sparky froze when it approached, chomped down on his ball, and walked away with his new prize. His owner saw that Sparky was after it and tossed it back to him. The mutt seemed friendly but didn't feel like giving up so easily. When Sparky took the ball, the mutt walked beside him and stuck his nose as close to the ball as possible. Sparky made it halfway back to us and froze again, the now slimy yellow orb barely wedged in his mouth. The mutt continued to sniff, and as I walked up I noticed that though he was motionless, Sparky was growling. He seemed to be telling the other dog, "Go away, freak! This is my ball!"

That's when I witnessed just how far his back streak could go. A strip of fur stood erect from his rear all the way up his neck. If he arched his back, he could almost be a cat. I came to realize that I could read his back like a kind of attitude thermometer or mood ring. I could decode his emotions if I read the signs correctly. Fur standing on his rear meant that he was nervous or excited. Fur raised from his bum to mid-back meant that he was very upset. A streak of disheveled fur from his tail to his neck was bad, like *DEFCON-1* bad, which meant that he was preparing for all-out war. If he stayed motionless, didn't wag his tail, and began growling, I could only expect the next move to be a pretty volatile one.

"Sparky, you need to learn to share," I said. Once I showed up, I began petting the mutt who wagged his tail happily. Sparky loosened up a little, but decided to retreat back to Allyson who was talking with our new friends. Just then, the mutt's owner came over and said, "Sorry about that. Beau loves tennis balls!"

"Oh no, it's fine," I said. "Sparky's got to learn how to get along with other dogs. This is a great way to help him do that."

We talked a few more minutes and then returned to our own group of friends. When I got back, Allyson was concerned, "It looked like Sparky was getting a little defensive out there."

"Yeah, he was," I said. "But when I showed up he relaxed some. It's all okay."

But Allyson was still worried. "Maybe we shouldn't throw the ball so far away while we're here. Looks like he could get into a scuffle with one of the bigger dogs."

I scanned the park and noticed how many large dogs were there, including the Doberman, a German Shepherd, a few Pit Bulls, and one gigantic Great Dane that probably had bowel movements larger than Sparky. "Yeah, good point," I said. "I'll keep Sparky nearby."

"That's a good idea," said one of our new friends. She was an older lady whose Bichon Frise sniffed around her feet. "A Dachshund was killed in here a few months ago, you know."

Allyson turned white, "What? How'd that happen?"

"Oh, it was terrible," she said. "The poor little thing was sniffing around the fence over there, when all of the sudden a bigger dog ran up and took it in its jaws and shook it like a rag doll—shook, shook, shook! The screaming was terrible! By the time it was over, the poor thing was dead. It was so awful. You'd better keep an eye on your little baby!"

I was a little stunned, mainly at how such a proper looking lady could tell a horrible story so effectively. "Yeah, let's keep Sparky close by. Where is he anyway?" I got a cold chill when I saw it.

A little boy had been throwing the ball with Sparky, and this time had thrown it across the field right into a pack of large dogs. Somehow, Sparky had gotten the ball but was frozen as three other big dogs were sniffing him all over. All of their tails slowed to a stop and the fur began to rise on their backs, too. Sparky must have been growling at them. This was *DEFCON 1* and something was about to snap. I knew he needed socializing, but with the proper lady's grotesque story fresh on my mind, I expected the worst. I knew that running over there could startle them all, so I started walking briskly. The other owners noticed too and began to call their dogs. No one moved. What the heck was going on?

That's when the Great Dane made his way over and startled the larger dogs. When they saw him, their ears dropped; and as he got closer, they ran away. Sparky remained frozen as the Dane jogged by, which freed him up to come back to us. On the way, another dog approached Sparky and the Dane showed up again to chase it away. It was as if he was looking out for Sparky. Such a cool scene!

We figured that had been enough excitement for one day. We took his gooey, grass-matted tennis ball from him, leashed him up, and led him to the car. Once inside, he jumped onto Allyson's lap. On the way home, he wasn't as interested in looking out the windows, but he did want to stare into the air conditioner vent for a while.

"You did so good Sparky! How did you like your first trip to the dog park?" Allyson asked. We could tell he was tired but content. "He got along pretty well with most of the dogs, don't you think?"

"Yeah," I said. "Except for the big ones. Sparky, you've got to learn that you're not as big and intimidating as you think you are. One day that growling you do is going to get you eaten."

"That's right, Sparky," Allyson said. "It's a good thing that Great Dane was around to look after you. Otherwise who knows what could have happened!"

HE'S A NATURAL GUARD DOG

I had been in graduate school for a year when Allyson and I got married, at which time I tried to take all the early morning courses I could so that I could work the afternoons and evenings. The schedule was rather easy for me since I had always been a morning person. Everyday Sparky and I snuck out of bed early, went potty, ate breakfast, and then he would lay next to my feet under a blanket to keep them warm while I read over the lecture notes for class that day. I normally studied every day for an hour before I had to get ready to leave. It was a good routine that Sparky and I followed for years.

My reading assignments included various sources, like the Bible, ancient Near Eastern texts, historiography, archeology, and linguistics—you know, the most exciting material possible that anyone could engage at 5 a.m. Since adopting Sparky, I started noticing that virtually all of the Bible texts had some rotten things to say about dogs. Some of the songwriters of the Hebrew Bible feared packs of wild dogs and related them to evil people. In fact, calling someone a dog was a supreme insult in those ancient settings. In fact, Goliath called David a dog during their legendary conflict. In the New Testament, Saint Paul called his opponents dogs. Even Jesus of Nazareth said that nobody should give holy things to dogs.

Thousands of wild dogs roamed the ancient world, which could be pretty scary when a pack of them showed up near a village. I thought about Sparky snoozing at my feet. *Dogs couldn't be all bad, could they?* As it turned out, there were a few positive references to dogs here and there. Apparently people used domesticated dogs for shepherding, and some scholars thought that Jesus was referring to dogs as pets at one point in the New Testament.*

All of these things had me wondering how dogs got to be so close to humans in the first place. Turns out, people had been domesticating dogs for several thousand years. Although there were no prehistoric wiener dogs to be found in the ancient fossil record (since they were bred much later), wolf-like dogs usually hung around some of the earliest human campsites and communities so that they could eat the scraps the people left. I'd seen dogs eat some putrid stuff, so I could see how having a pack of living garbage disposals just outside your campsite would be beneficial. On top of that, dogs acted as a good protection to the community, barking and howling at any peculiar noises they heard nearby. So prehistoric dogs acted as garbage disposals and alarm systems. Not a bad deal for the humans.

Trying to make sense of my research, I imagined a very hairy caveman falling asleep with a fire on one side and his slightly less-hairy female companion on the other. As he drifts off, he thinks about how great those four-legged things outside the camp are, eating his trash and alerting him of danger. So he thinks he'll train the dogs to do much more like pulling carts, attacking bad guys, and fetching his cowhide sandals.

But little does our prehistoric man know that his favorite bear rug would develop mysterious wet spots and start to smell like urine. Those things happen when you get new dogs.

Though Sparky had little in common with the wolf-like canines of the past, he did like to bark. In fact, he barked at everything. The neighbors upstairs would make noise, and he'd bark. He'd hear a car alarm, and he'd bark. He heard birds chirping outside—bark. I opened a soda can—bark. I belched—bark. Sometimes Sparky heard something really unusual, like the sound of a baby cooing in its mother's arms as she walks by our apartment door. Sparky found these kinds of sounds so unnerving that he would bark like a lunatic, charge the door, and do a tribal war dance.

Truthfully, Sparky wasn't as tough as I had originally thought. Sure he had an attitude at times, but it was more for show. I'd wager that if I actually opened the door and showed him the cute little baby he wanted to charge, he'd retreat in a droopy-eared, tail-tucked panic. It disappointed me at first, but I figured a tough looking dog that wouldn't hurt a fly was much better than any other dog that could eat a stranger's leg and cost Allyson and I a sizable lawsuit. Let him bark, as long as he didn't bite.

And bark he did. So much so, we had a few more nicknames for him: *Sparky-Barky* or just *Barky*. I even tried calling him *Bob Barker* for a little while, telling Allyson it fit best since Sparky had been neutered. She didn't go for that at all, but did agree that all the barking was annoying. When I relayed my new understanding of how prehistoric man found dogs valuable because of their ability to consume trash and bark at noises, Allyson gave me a blank stare and said, "Do you have some kind of geek button I can push to turn that side of you off?"

"Sorry babe. The geek never turns off," I said with a snort-laugh and pushed my glasses up the bridge of my nose.

Not only was I in touch with my inner nerd, I was also channeling the spirit of my Neolithic ancestors. I had found great value in my little dog's maniacal tirades and thought about how it made our home virtually impenetrable. While Allyson and I were away, I was certain a thief would steer clear of the apartment sheltering a barking dog. I also felt a keen sense of security while at home. If a car alarm sounded in the distance, we would know about it before that poor car-owner would. Mischievous birds outside our window, beware! We're already savvy to your plans of home invasion. And to all of those cute, gurgling toddlers thinking about busting down our front door, just know that our weenie dog stands at the ready, so do your worst!

Maybe I was channeling more of Sparky's spirit.

****

It was fall and the weather had gotten pretty chilly. True to Allyson's prediction, Sparky had become better than an electric blanket, always preferring to sit between us when we watched a movie. If he wasn't playing ball, you could bet he was looking for a place to take a nap, and that involved burrowing underneath anything he could find. If there was a blanket on the floor, Sparky could be hidden in one of the folds. I learned quickly that I couldn't fall into a pile of pillows without first checking for lumps, since Sparky saw it as the perfect napping fortress. Not much of a fortress when I came crashing down, mind you. And I can't tell how many times I found him ensconced in a pile of laundry fresh out of the drier. I'd pour the load out onto the couch, put the laundry basket up, and come back to a mound of whites or colors pulsating with life as Sparky had already dug his way to the center. He may have put off tons of heat, but really he was cold natured and would do anything to stay warm.

That worked out well for us on the cold nights watching TV under a blanket, though there were a few problems. First of all, Sparky liked to lick everything around him. When he wasn't chasing a toy, he held it between his paws so that he could chew and lick it. It was, I suppose, how he passed the time. Unfortunately, he would get under a blanket with us and lick whatever was in front of him: a foot, an arm, a leg, a hand, the couch. We told him *no* which sometimes put an end to it. But once he shifted to another position, he was compelled to lick again. More than once, we'd try to lie down on the couch and squish into an area soaked in Sparky spittle. Gross.

Another problem was how moody the sleeping weenie got when we tried to move him. It was actually more comical than problematic. We could nudge him and he'd stay quiet, but if we tried to shove him, say to the other side of the couch, it pissed him off. It was always a tame growl, as if he was saying *Go away! Sleeping!* It usually happened while he was snoozing beside us in bed, and we'd just ignore the grump.

Yes, he still slept in the bed with us at night. We had decided to give it a few weeks and try making him a spot on the floor again, but we got as used to things as he did and forgot about it. The fact that he put off so much heat made it quite nice sometimes even though we were still pretty cramped in the full-sized bed. He wasn't really a team player when it came to sleeping etiquette, giving a growl every time we moved him. We'd just ignore it and move on.

One evening we awoke to a startling shout outside our window: "Hey you! Stop! Thief!" I looked over at the clock: 2:45 a.m. Getting jolted out of our deep sleep threw Allyson and I somewhere between groggyness and panic. Our hearts were racing as we tried to figure out what to do. We didn't know what was going on, so decided not to call the police yet. Thinking we could have been robbed, I looked around the house to make sure everything was okay. I checked the front door, windows, and the sliding glass door to our balcony. Everything was secure. Since we lived on the second floor, I really didn't think much about the windows, but they were all locked anyway.

"What about our cars?" Allyson asked.

"I'm not worried about the cars as much," I said. "It sounded like it came from the woods, not the parking lot." The back of our apartment building faced a quaint creek hidden in a deep wooded area. It was a beautiful place during the day, but became unsettling at night since it seemed to swallow the outside lights completely as one wandered from the building. But to be thorough, I threw on shorts and shirt and ran down the stairs to check the cars. The parking lot was well lit as usual, and our cars remained untouched.

Were we dreaming? Did we really even hear someone shouting? It seemed so near, as if it was just outside our bedroom window; but that didn't make sense. The fact that nobody else in the complex was up and checking their own things was even more surreal. Allyson and I talked it over a few more minutes, and since all of our things were secure, we decided just to go back to sleep.

About twenty minutes later, we were roused again —this time by a flashlight shinning into our bedroom window. We could hear a couple of guys talking outside in normal voices. Since they were so non-chalant about it, I opened the window and said, "Can I help you?"

"Sir, I'm with the Dallas Police," said the man with the flashlight. "Do you have any bicycles on your balcony?"

"Yes sir, we have two," I said.

Another voice, the guy next to the officer said, "You don't anymore!"

Stunned, I said, "What…? What the heck is going on?"

The man continued, "Somebody stole my racing bikes off my balcony. When I got home I saw him on yours and tried to scare him off. But it looks like he got yours, too."

"Who is it?" Allyson asked. "What are they saying?"

"It's the police, and one of our neighbors," I told her. "They say our bikes are gone!"

Allyson gasped. "Someone's been on our balcony? Are you sure they're gone?"

"Uhh...." I turned to the window and shouted down, "Are you sure they're gone?"

"I saw the guy run off with your bike," said one of the figures. "Nobody's up there now. We'll watch while you check, if you want."

First, I shined my own light down to see the guy's uniform, then turned on the balcony lights and peeked out the blinds. I was relieved to see that there was no intruder and furious that there were also no bikes either. We *had* stored our two mountain bikes out there with no chain or lock to secure them. Really, we didn't see the need to go that extra step, never dreaming that someone would climb up and take them.

Allyson and I got dressed and stepped outside to file a report with the police. They told us they would do their best, but stolen bikes really weren't high on their priority list. Translation: the bikes were gone forever. Over a thousand dollars down the drain. But that wasn't as bad as our neighbor's loss, who lived on the third floor one building over. He was on a professional racing team and had two bikes that represented a loss of nearly three thousand dollars. He had just come home from bar tending and noticed his bikes were missing. While he was on the phone with the police, he saw the culprit lowering a bike down from our balcony. It seemed he climbed up on his own and took a rope with him for each bike that he used to lower them down. Then he'd climb down and ride his new bikes to safety. Our neighbor saw the thief, shouted at him, and chased him as far as he could. The police arrived soon after.

It was 3:30 a.m. when we finished the police report and got back into bed. With a long sigh of relief

I spread out under the sheets and tried to forget the whole evening, hoping to get a few hours of sleep in before morning. But a shifting lump under the sheets growled at me before I could dose off; I just woke Sparky.

I threw the covers off him and just stared him down. His eyes made it clear that he was just as annoyed as I was. "Sparky!" I said, "You'd bark your head off if a gnat farts! But you can't even let us know when a burglar climbs on our balcony and steals our bikes? What's the matter with you? He could have made a sandwich in the kitchen and you'd still be out cold!"

Unimpressed and still groggy, he dropped his head back down and closed his eyes. *So much for our guard dog,* I thought. I covered him back up with a grimace and turned off the lights. After a moment of silence I said, "Maybe we should think about a security system at our next place."

HE'S FINE BY HIMSELF

Though he wasn't exactly guard-dog material, Sparky had proven to be the perfect dog for us. He was small, reasonably obedient, and eager to please. He only occasionally made mistakes on the floor, but peed on command when we took him outside—a benefit that proved useful for us all. Sparky made us very happy, which is why I was floored when Allyson wanted to get another dog, and it had to be a female. I suppose she felt there was too much testosterone in the house. She argued that we were five states away from her family where she lived with her mom and sister for years, and now felt like she was sort of outvoted. Two males and one female in the house represented a kind of imbalance of power.

This somehow meant that Sparky had a vote on things. I think that was news to him. If he ever came to realize that he had that kind of influence, I doubt he would ever vote for the guys. Anyone who throws his ball a few times in the back yard could sway the ballot at any moment. An extra treat here and there, more afternoon walks—yeah, Sparky's swing vote could make him alpha of our home faster than he could drag his rear on the carpet. So I got it, Allyson wanted a girl dog, but did that really justify getting two dogs?

"It's not just that," she said. "Sparky needs company while we're at work. I hate to think of him cooped up all day while we are away."

Yeah okay, that made sense. Allyson and I were living on the second floor of a three-story apartment where the neighbors were noisy and sometimes downright rambunctious. It would be as quiet as a mouse until *BOOM!* It freaked us out, especially Sparky who barked at everything except burglars. I could only imagine how hard it would be on him while he was alone during the day. He already had a tough time being fenced in, but when you added the rumbles from above, the murmurings below, and the occasional siren and car alarm outside, I would wager it was tough on the little guy.

But I resisted. "We've got one dog already, Allyson. That's plenty for us! I think two dogs would be too much right now, at least while we are in such a small apartment. You know, it's already a chore taking Sparky out four times a day with the stairs and all. Can you imagine doing that with two dogs?"

Every time I had to take Sparky out, I carried him down the long apartment stairs. His midget legs and long back made it nearly impossible for him manage stairs on his own. So when we went out I took the poop bag, the leash, and Sparky in my arms. Most of the time only one of us took Sparky out to go potty, and it always required both hands. I imagined that if we added another dog to the scenario, things would get pretty hairy. I supposed I could put a dog in each arm, but what if I tripped on the way down? With just Sparky, I could use my free arm to catch the handrail. But with two dogs, we'd all take a fifteen-foot tumble down the concrete stairs in front of our door. That was sure to do damage to *all* our backs. When I explained it to Allyson, she understood but gave one more point to consider.

"I know it will be a little more work, but I'm worried about him. Most days he's cooped up in the kitchen for several hours. I just don't want him to become like that first dog we had."

Aw crap! I forgot about Cujo! My face turned a little white. We had seen firsthand what happened to a dog left at home all day with no interaction, and it freaked us out. Allyson and I both wondered if our sweet little Sparky-dog would eventually undergo a similar transformation into a furry little chainsaw roaring around us, trying to chew up friends and visitors. I saw a glimpse of the future at that point: Sparky attached to my neighbor's leg snarling and growling while I try to pry him off saying, "He really *is* a good dog!"

That did it. I was convinced it was time to find Sparky some company and we began searching the newspapers and Internet for anyone who sold Dachshunds. We considered getting another kind of dog, but Sparky was so great we figured another Dachshund would be the perfect companion. We didn't care about breeding them and just thought that another miniature weenie dog would be the best match.

Allyson and I thumbed through the yellow pages and found an entry that caught our attention: *Champion Dachshund Breeders: over 35 years of experience.* It sounded good, so I gave the number a call and spoke a few minutes with the owner. When he said hello I could hear the yipping of several little dogs in the background. His name was William, but he insisted that I call him Bill. He had a high baritone voice that was louder than normal, maybe to compensate for the constant yipping he heard. I told him that we were looking for a female Dachshund.

"Oh greeeaaat!" His voice was a pleasant song. "I happen to have more girls than boys right now, so you're in luck! Which color do you prefer?"

"Well, we hadn't really thought that far ahead. My wife and I have a red Dachshund right now and need another one to keep him company."

"The ones I have are all short-haired. I have mostly reds, some black-and-tans, and one dappled. The dappled is gorgeous and she's a girl, too! Why don't you come by and see what we have?"

I told him how much we were looking to spend and he assured me that we could work something out. I made an appointment for Allyson and me to meet him at his home the next Saturday afternoon. When I hung up, I grinned at Allyson.

"We have an appointment with Bill the Breeder."

****

That Saturday, we pinned up Sparky in the kitchen and told him that we were going to get him a sister. His reaction was the same as always, constant barking and jumping as we made our way out the door. It was about a forty-minute drive to Bill's home in a prominent upper-middle class neighborhood. We gawked at his nicely kempt yard and long driveway just down the cul-de-sac which made us dream out loud about what we'd like in our own future home. Parking on the street, we made our way up the sidewalk to the front door, noting along the way that this home must have had twice as many flowers as the others on the block. Bill obviously took great pride in his home.

There was a large, bulbous, golden knocker on the center of the front door that seemed out of place. It was disproportionate to the door and rather gaudy. I looked at Allyson with a small grin and whispered, "That's a big one!" She giggled as I gave it three knocks and stepped back. We heard the sound of the dogs yipping somewhere in the house. A few moments later, we heard the locks unlatch and the door opened to reveal a short, rotund man who greeted us with an enthusiastic "Helllllo!" It was Bill the Breeder.

Bill must have been in his sixties with a bright personality and welcoming demeanor. He was wearing a multi-colored button-up shirt that was tucked into his deep blue jeans. When he shook my hand, I noticed that he wore several gold rings that matched the color of the chain around his neck. His top two shirt buttons were undone revealing a sparkling pendant hovering just above his silvery chest hair. His groomed mustache made crisp, white points at the corners of his mouth, and his silver hair was thin but well controlled with pomade. It was glassy and immovable, perfectly parted to the left in one stylistic wave.

He welcomed us in and led us down the hallway into his living room. The walls were covered with several pictures of Dachshunds standing beside their proud owners. Bill talked about them as we made our way. These were the dogs that he bred. He was very proud of them all and had a special relationship with their owners. We took a seat in a spacious living room and admired the pictures as he continued to tell us his story. Adornments of all sorts seemed to overpower the room.

Bill had been a breeder for decades, explaining that his dogs were exceptional since they had won multiple awards. But he still kept his costs reasonable so that average folks could own these great dogs. The fact that we were looking for a female meant that the price was higher. I didn't really understand the reasoning but it made Allyson and I worried. Maybe we really didn't have the money for a girl dog after all.

"Why don't I bring them out so you can meet them all?" he said.

"You want to bring them out here in your living room?" Allyson said. "I thought we would just go to the back and see them."

"Oh, no! It's much better this way! It gives them the chance to approach you instead of the other way around. Makes them more comfortable. Gives them time to get used to you."

We agreed and Bill disappeared down another hallway. Then we heard him yell, "Here they come!" It sounded like a hundred stampeding Lilliputians tearing down the hallway. About ten miniature Dachshund puppies ran out to greet us, tongues hanging to the side, ears flopping all over, and all the happy yipping! Allyson and I were sitting on the floor when they fumbled over both of us, licking and sniffing like crazy. I believe that everyone should be charged by a bunch of love-crazed puppies at least once in life. It was awesome.

Bill had an uncanny knowledge of his dogs. He introduced them all and included the history for each one. True to his earlier description, there were mostly reds, a few black-and-tans, and one dapple spotted from head to toe with white, black, and grey spots. She was the cutest, but there was no way we could afford her.

A true salesman, he let us pick out a favorite female and then named his price. Even after we worked him down some, it was out of our budget. While Allyson and Bill chatted, an especially long, especially pudgy black-and-tan pup caught my eye. I don't know what it was about him, but I liked him. Maybe it was the fact that, though he liked to play with the others, he spent most of his time exploring the room. *I'm with you there, Kiddo,* I thought. *There's plenty in here to look at!* His desire to explore things appealed to my scholarly nature, and he had a different look about him that impressed me, too.

We narrowed down our choices to three dogs. Two of them were red females, and one of them was the black-and-tan male that I adored. When it was decision time, we just didn't have the money for the girls, so Allyson suggested that we look somewhere else. But I couldn't let go of the male.

"We're here for a girl dog!" Allyson said.

"I know, I know, but we don't have the money for these girls."

"Well, let's just look somewhere else, then."

But I couldn't. "I really like that black one over there. Why don't we get him?"

At that moment, he looked me right in the eye. There was a strong psychic link between us both. Then he urinated. Even though he just made it tougher to make my case, I couldn't help but laugh.

"He just *peed!* Right there! You really want *that* one?" Allyson said, eyes wide open. "We could have gotten a Cocker Spaniel if that's your thing. They pee everywhere!"

"Yeah! He's a rebel. That's all. He'll be great! I know it!"

"But, he's fat!"

"That's nothing! It's just baby fat! He can lose that in no time!"

"We'll have to put him on a diet!"

Beaming, I said, "So you're thinking about it, huh?"

Allyson just stared back fighting a grin, one eyebrow raised.

Knock! Knock! Knock! The front door creaked open. "Hello! It's just me!"

"Oh hi, Rich! Come on in," Bill said. "Rich, I'd like you to meet our two new customers, Jason and Allyson. Jason and Allyson, this is my friend Richard. We've worked together for many years."

He greeted us both with a gentle handshake, "Please, just call me Rich."

Like Bill, Rich was probably in his sixties. He was tall, lean and a little lanky. He wore a pair of blue shorts, sandals, and a sleeveless denim vest. He didn't have as many rings as Bill, but did wear a large gold chain around his neck, which rested comfortably on a bed of silver chest hair pouring out of his unbuttoned vest collar. Cleanly shaven, Rich had a full head of thick, shiny gray hair that swirled in an Elvis-like fashion, some strands of his bangs curling down his forehead. As we talked, he lit a cigarette holding it with his index finger and thumb, crossed his legs in a European fashion and bobbed a sandal up and down with his toes.

Bill excused himself for a moment, so we continued to chat with Rich.

"So how long have you and Bill been breeding?" I realized what I'd said and tried to recover. "I mean, how long have you both been in the dog business?" I could just begin to feel the beads of sweat forming on my forehead.

Thankfully, Rich didn't make it a big deal. "Oh, Bill and I have worked together for several years. I connected with him after retiring some years ago. We've learned a lot together. It's been a fun ride."

He asked us if we'd decided on a dog yet, so we told him our dilemma. We came to get a girl dog as a companion for Sparky, but it looked like a boy dog is all we could afford.

"Do you want to breed the dogs?" he asked.

"No, not at all," Allyson said. "Whichever dog we adopt is getting fixed. I've always wanted a girl dog, but the main reason we want another one is to keep Sparky company when we are away."

"Well then, since you are not worried about mating them, either a male or female will do. Their temperaments may be a little different, but no matter which you choose, they'll find a way to work it out. They'll find a way to become family. We've seen it time and time again. Don't worry so much about that, just choose the one you want and go for it."

I looked at Allyson with a goofy smile. She looked back at me, grinned, shrugged, and caved.

"You really like this one, don't you?" she said.

"I really do."

"He's kinda growing on me, too."

Even though Allyson had her heart set on a girl dog, she had to admit that the black one was nice and would still be good company for Sparky. So after we coaxed and teased each other some more, we both agreed that we'd get the black-and-tan pudgy pee-er. We paid our dues and signed the paperwork, thanked Bill and Rich, put the puppy in our car, and started our way home.

On the road, we wondered what we'd name him. Bill said that he was a little plumper than the other dogs because he had been taking medicine covered in gobs of peanut butter. Back in the car, Allyson held our new furry black-and-tan addition and said, "You've got lots of peanut butter inside you, don't you? You know, you're even the color of peanut butter and chocolate—like a Reese's Peanut Butter Cup!"

The name stuck like peanut butter, too. When we got home, we introduced Sparky to Reesie.

HE LOVES US BOTH THE SAME

Sparky wasn't as happy about Reesie as we thought he'd be. We expected him to welcome the new addition, but his reaction was more like "Who the heck is this intruder?" A new dog that came into his home, chewing on his toys, drinking out of his water bowl, and taking the attention of his humans was a lot for him to digest. So Sparky growled at Reesie from time to time, reminding him who really owned our home, who was the original Garrison weenie dog.

But Reesie wasn't wound up as tight as Sparky. A lover more than a fighter, he liked playing with the plush toys and sporadically charging around the house, but overall he preferred exploring every nook and cranny in the apartment or simply getting a rubdown. Both of them needed to be touching us wherever we were. You could bet a dog would be at your feet while at the desk or lying against your hip on the couch. We couldn't even escape them in the bathroom. Being on the other side of any door was totally unacceptable.

Since they were both stuck with each other all of the time, Sparky learned to tolerate Reesie more and more. He growled when Reesie touched him, and Reesie would freeze until Sparky was finished. But as soon as Sparky hunkered down for a nap, the puppy would find some way to touch him. Sparky would awaken to Reesie's back against his. If Reesie was asleep, Sparky didn't see any need to complain. Later, he'd find Reesie had rested his head on his rump, then on his ribs—inching closer each time. It wore Sparky down until he finally accepted Reesie completely and proved that even Sparky was no match for puppy love.

While Sparky's potty training was a breeze, Ressie's took a lot more patience. I don't think Bill did any training with him, so we had to start from scratch. The first time I caught him peeing in the house was while he was on one of his little explorations. He was under the dining room table and decided to drop right there and go. There's the rebel that first caught my attention! Before he could finish, I crept up behind him and took hold of his mane. I scared the wits out of the poor pup. I think he nearly had a heart attack, yelping and howling even though I didn't hurt him at all. Allyson rushed into the room asking if I stepped on the little tyke. "No," I said, "He peed, and I just grabbed him and he freaked out."

Consequently, that was our first lesson in Reesie's absentmindedness. When he was exploring, he would shut the rest of the world out completely. We'd let him roam a little outside without his leash, where he would catch a scent and track it indefinitely until something physically stopped him. Oftentimes, he would ignore us completely and lose track of where he was. We'd almost lost him more than once since he wouldn't even respond to our calls. Although, one word did seem to rouse him: *treat*. If we said, "You wanna treat?" his ears went up like doggie radar and he'd come running. But not even the promise of food could stop him if the scent he was on was strong enough, and we'd have to chase him down. Needless to say, we kept him leashed most of the time.

That was one of the things that frustrated Allyson so much about Reesie. She was already a little agitated that our second dog was a boy instead of the girl that she wanted initially. Without question, the boys now had the majority vote. On top of that, Reesie tended to like me more than her. He'd go where I went, lay on my lap, fetch the toys that I threw for him, and was generally more excited to see me when I came home from work. While watching TV in the evenings, he'd fall asleep on my lap while Allyson sat with folded arms at the other side of the couch.

One evening she blurted out, "You suck, you know that?" She glared at Reesie and I, her arms still tightly folded.

"Who are you talking to?" I asked. "Me or Reesie?" Reesie had just woken up; and since I was looking at Allyson, he looked at Allyson.

"Both of you!" she said. "Why does he love you more than me? It's been weeks and he wants nothing to do with me! Have you been feeding him treats behind my back?"

"What? He doesn't hate you. How do you figure that?" I thought this was one of those *does-this-dress-make-me-look-fat?* conversations. I knew that she had a point, but I didn't want simply to agree. Not if I wanted to sleep in the same bed with her that night, anyway.

She continued, "Well for starters, he's chewed holes in my shoes, two of my purses, and about five pairs of my socks! He hasn't eaten *any* of your stuff."

"Not yet, but I'm sure he'll get to something of mine eventually. I guess he just likes the way you smell." I had no idea what I was talking about, but felt like I had to justify Reesie's desire to eat Allyson's things somehow.

"Whatever! Yesterday, he even pooped in the bedroom on my side of the bed. He's never done that on your side!"

"There could be a thousand reasons for that, Ally! Maybe he smells something on the floor that's drawing him over there."

Allyson just shook it off and slowly unrolled her arm, pointing her supine hand at me. "And look at *this!* He's on your lap every night, but he won't even come near me. Do you have liver treats in your pocket or something?"

"Well, listen," I was determined to patch this up, "Sparky is more of *your* dog, but Reesie was *my* choice. So he's more mine. That may explain why Reesie is on my lap more."

"Oh really? And where is Sparky right now?" she asked. I looked down to find Sparky on the cushion between us. He had been sleeping, but now he was sitting there awake with tremors at about a category 4. He always trembled when Allyson and I had our more passionate conversations.

"There, see?" Allyson said. "He's between us, not on my lap. He wants to touch us *both*. He responds to us *both*. He gets excited when *either one of us* spends time with him. He loves us *both*. Reesie adores you, and only you. It's not right! I'm the one who lived with dogs all my life. I'm the one who wanted dogs, and the second one that we get doesn't even like me."

"Honey, both of the dogs love you, especially Sparky. He'll get in your lap right now, won't you Spar-" But Sparky was gone. In the blink of an eye he had sneaked away to his hideout underneath our bed. He could only take so much of our raised voices; it was always like that. I saw Allyson's composure break for a second to giggle at Sparky's retreat.

"Allyson, why don't you take Reesie," I said, and carefully placed the black dog on her lap. She smiled and began to scratch Reesie behind the ears—his favorite spot. He indulged for a few seconds, but once he saw me he crawled my way again. Allyson took him in a bear hug and tried everything to regain his attention, drowning him in coos, kisses, and rubs. Though he was immobile, he wouldn't take his eyes off of me. I even gestured the *stay* command, though he hadn't learned it yet, but it only made him start barking at me. "Fine!" Allyson said, releasing him. He darted over and nuzzled his way into my lap again. I shrugged.

"You think we can return this dog, too?" she asked. I thought she was joking. Maybe.

"We can't give him up! He's awesome!" I said.

"Yeah, yeah. You know if we got a girl dog, this wouldn't have happened."

"Right, then you'd have a dog that loved you more than me, and the tables would be turned. How is that fair?"

"But you wouldn't care as much as I do about this. You would have been happy if we didn't even get a dog," she said.

Yeah, that was true.

"Look, I just can't help the way it is," I said. "Give it time, I know he'll warm up to you."

"Sure. Whatever," she said, her tone now subdued. "Well, I'm gong to bed." She leaned over and lightly kissed Reesie on his furry nose. "Goodnight, you stupid dog. You'd better start liking me soon."

When Allyson went into the bedroom, I had a heart-to-heart with the pup: "Reesie, I think you'd better break the ice with Mommy, because that sounded a little ominous."

****

Routinely, Reesie came to bed the same way Sparky did. He'd lay with us (actually, *me*) while we read; but before we turned out the lights, Reesie went into the travel kennel that we had previously bought for Sparky. We were told that kind of kennel training was great for the dogs that would come to see the kennel as a kind of security blanket. Of course, Reesie whined when I placed him in it, but soon accepted it as his bed in just a few nights with no problems. We wished that Sparky could have made such an easy transition, but he made a terrible fuss each time we tried.

When Allyson and I left the dogs alone during the day, they both went into the kitchen behind the baby gate. Though he also barked at us as we left, Reesie had no problem staying there. After a few weeks, he'd rarely bark at us when we left, mainly because we promised him a treat if he went into the kitchen willingly. I'd say "You wanna go in the kitchen?" and he'd look at me like I just promised him the master key to Purina, darting into the kitchen as fast as his stumpy legs could take him. He'd wait just behind the open baby gate where I could give him a liver treat, his whole elongated body squirming in an effort to make his already wagging tail go faster. He also showed us a happy-hop, which was just his front paws popping off the ground over and over while his rear stayed snuggly on the floor. I showed him the treat, and his eyes locked on the target. If I hesitated or asked him if he wanted it, he'd begin to bark with his body squirming and hopping erratically. His bark was delightful and unusual, like the chirp a car's tire makes when a driver pops the clutch. He only barked like this when he was really excited, or anytime food was nearby.

Once Reesie got his treat, he accepted the fact that we'd be gone a few hours. Sparky, on the other hand, heard our command to get into the kitchen and retreated to his hideaway. Though we were pretty sure that Reesie would sell his soul for a liver treat, Sparky would rather we stay home forever. Once we swept him out of his cave, I'd place him behind the baby gate with Reesie where he accosted us with barks just as he touched the floor. He'd accept the treat as a formality: *Fine. I'll eat it, but I won't like it.* Sometimes Reesie would start barking too, but I think he was just trying to fit in.

Just about everyone was delighted to meet Sparky and Reesie, but they always gave Reesie special attention because he was still a puppy. When we were out for a walk, people in the neighborhood often came over to say hello to the young weenie. One of my brothers, Lance, planned to visit us from Alabama for a few days, and we wanted Reesie to be as trained as possible. So, we taught him the tricks that Sparky already knew. In a desperate move to win Reesie's attention, Allyson volunteered to be his trainer. In no time, Reesie learned to sit, shake, roll over, speak, and—the climax—be a bear. Being a bear was the biggest challenge for Reesie since he was considerably longer than Sparky, but he was determined to master it. Besides, that dog would do anything for a liver treat. And even though Allyson was concerned about Reesie's ballooning gut, I think she snuck him more treats than usual to bribe him for affection.

When Lance arrived, we lined the two dogs up who demonstrated the tricks without missing a beat. Afterwards, it was time for me to take the dogs for a walk. Lance offered to take one of them down the stairs, but I wanted to show him how I managed on my own. I sat at the top of the long flight of stairs and the two dogs approached me immediately, one at my left hip and the other at my right. I hooked each of their collars to their own retractable leash and put each leash handle in my pants pocket. Then I scooped Reesie up in my right arm and Sparky up in my left and walked down the stairs. It was a bit of a circus act, but the dogs' short legs straddled my forearms perfectly and my hands always got a firm grip under their barrel chests, which gave me terrific control. Once I reached ground level, I squatted down and they'd hop right out of my arms and off we'd go for a walk. Lance was impressed. When we came back, Sparky tore up the stairs, but Reesie wasn't ready for such a large flight. It took him some time before he could manage them on his own, so I'd usually carry him up myself. This time, Lance was eager to take him.

Reesie liked Lance immediately and jumped into his lap as soon as possible. I was surprised at how fast it happened. It was just more evidence that Reesie was a lover and not a fighter. Lance would pet Reesie while catching us up on his life and occasionally stop stroking, which was when Reesie would stick his nose under Lance's hand and nudge it back on top of his head.

"Did you see that?" Lance said with a laugh. "He doesn't want me to stop!"

"He really likes you, Lance," I said.

Allyson chuckled. "He *does* like you, and you just got here, too." Her tone was a little snarky.

Lance liked both our dogs but found Reesie to be a little strange. When he'd play with them on the floor, Reesie was engaged for a little while until he caught an interesting scent. In the middle of a tug-a-rope battle, his nose would go wild and he'd just leave with his snout to the ground. Throw a ball for him to fetch and he'd bring it back until one throw sent him to a corner of the apartment that he felt needed more exploring, then he'd disappear. "Where'd he go?" Lance asked getting up to investigate. He'd find Reesie in the dining room sleuthing out a trail or in the bedroom nosing around the dirty clothes hamper. One time, he found Reesie snorting and licking wildly at some crumb under the oven that was just out of reach.

Since we were still potty training Reesie, we had to take him out more than Sparky. Lance was kind enough to help during his visit. One day he took Reesie out and was gone a little longer than usual. When the door opened, Reesie, happy as usual, ran inside. Lance followed wearing a weird smirk: "I'm sorry to have to tell you this, but your dog is an idiot."

"I'm not surprised," Allyson said. "Why? What happened?"

"While we were walking around on the grass I stopped and gave him plenty of slack on the leash so that he could find a place to relieve himself. Well, he didn't do that, but he did find a nice cushy ant bed to sit on."

"Oh no!" Allyson said. "Did he get bitten?"

"I don't think so. I pulled him off as soon as I saw it, and looked all over him for ants. He had a few on him but they were on his fur. I don't think any of them got him."

We looked Reesie over to make sure he was all right; of course he sat in my lap in the process. Allyson made sure I noticed. We all got a laugh out of the whole ant-bed thing. It was more evidence that Reesie was a one-track-minded dog that didn't pay a lot of attention to his surroundings.

While Lance was in town, he and I went out a lot to do guy stuff that Allyson wasn't interested in. It was a win for Allyson too since it gave her some exclusive time with Reesie. When Lance left for home, I helped him take his bags to his car, said goodbye, and watched him drive away. I came back inside and found Allyson on the couch with Sparky on her lap…and Reesie, too. I smiled and sat next to them. Sparky moved over to my lap, but Reesie was far too comfortable to budge. Allyson wore the brightest smile and let out a happy whisper: "Yay!" Finally, Reesie and Allyson had a bond.

Looking back on things, I suppose that Reesie was used to being around guys. His two previous owners were men after all, which explained why he easily accepted Lance and me, but was hesitant with Allyson. Now everything was cool. Later, Reesie even preferred

Allyson over me, but it always balanced itself out in the long run. Even though both dogs accepted us, from that point on we called Sparky Allyson's dog and Reesie my dog. Those designations usually came up when one of the dogs did something embarrassing. For some reason, most of those stories came from my dog.

A NEUTERED DOG HAS NO PASSION

As Sparky grew, his looks became more mature and distinguished. A shorthaired Dachshund, his fur was thin and red, which made things simple for brushing, though he was still a very soft dog. He had a stout chest, long back, and thin waist, not really fitting the sausage-like features we expected from a weenie dog. Surprisingly, he got even faster as he grew into adulthood and retained his fanatical love of squeaky toys and tennis balls.

Reesie, on the other hand, changed dramatically as he grew. It was surprising because of the clear changes to his body, but also because we expected he would become a fine specimen when he matured. He was the offspring of award-winning dogs, after all. But after the first months of owning him, we could tell that Reesie was going to be quite different from Sparky. If it weren't for his protruding, peanut butter induced belly, his trunk would resemble a long sausage link. His black and tan fir was much thicker and softer than Sparky's, and he seemed to know it gave him powers over anyone who tried to resist petting him. A couple of strokes, and just about anyone would invite him onto his or her lap. His ears were wider and longer than Sparky's, nearly reaching the tip of his nose—an attractive trait, but they often got dirty and needed lots of cleaning.

Other features seemed comically disproportionate to the rest of him. Allyson noticed that his front paws were much bigger than Sparky's, but his back paws remained a more normal size. And about those back legs, the poor dog was bowlegged. I'd be on my stomach playing with him with my cheek on the floor, and crack up when I saw his floppy front paws walk by followed by his dainty pigeon-toed tootsies. Then I'd see his tail way after he had walked past, it was bushy and almost as long as his back. Even though he tended to get lost on his sporadic explorations, we could always bet that the happy dog would be wagging his tail. So all we'd have to do was listen for the sound of it hammering against something: *Bap! Bap! Bap!* Lucky for him the peculiar amount of fur on his tail provided some form of protection against injury. And his back—good grief! The dog's back seemed a mile long! It was as if he had a few extra vertebrae in there.

The traits that made him a little odd also made him more adorable. Unfortunately, some of them made him more prone to injury or illness. Not long after getting him, we took him to the vet for shots and a check up, and took Sparky along for his own exam. The vet told us that Reesie's extra-long back combined with his hefty gut made him more prone to back injuries. Also, his crazy rear legs could pose their own problems, and we'd have to make sure his droopy ears stayed clean and dry to prevent infections. As for Sparky's check up, the trim and athletic dog got another clean bill of health.

When we went to the desk to pay, I remembered how much of a pain it was to cut Sparky's nails and asked if the vet techs could take care of it.

"No problem. It should only take a minute," one of them said and took our docile red dog to the room directly at the end of the hallway. Allyson and I didn't bother sitting down. Besides, by standing we could see through a small window into Sparky's room, and I wanted to see how the professionals clipped the nails of a difficult dog. I'm glad we watched, because we learned a lot.

First, one tech went into the room with Sparky. Then she stuck her head out and asked for someone to give her a hand. A few minutes later, we heard a call over the intercom and two more people went in. When the door opened, I caught a glimpse of Sparky wearing a bright green muzzle.

I laughed, "So that's how it's done! Four techs and a muzzle—the professional method." Suddenly, I felt pretty good about my struggles to cut Sparky's nails on my own.

****

Though the dogs dreaded trips to the vet, playing a game of fetch once we got home cheered them up right away. Sparky was the best at it, bringing back a tossed tennis ball immediately after each throw. But we had to play diligently, or else. If we didn't throw the ball again, he'd bark out his complaints. If we continued to ignore him, he'd happily chew the yellow fuzz off the ball bit by bit and later gag up awful piles of yellow fuzz and bile around the house. Note to self: tennis balls were for throwing, and squeak toys were for chewing. Unfortunately, his Babies was no more, missing in action while staying at a friend's house. Instead, we replaced it with a honking stuffed mole that became his "Mo-Mo." I can't remember who gave it that ridiculous name. It must have been Allyson.

Reesie cared little for tennis balls, though he did occasionally chase a tossed squeaky toy until a curious scent sidetracked him. Unlike Lance, I was wise to his spontaneous explorations. If he disappeared after I tossed a toy, I'd sneak up behind him and scare him, scratching his rear wildly while making monkey sounds. He'd snap out of his little world of exploration with a jump, his tail tucked, back arched, and stumpy little legs a blur beneath him. It made me laugh every time, but I'm sure Allyson laughed more at the black weenie dog running from the two-hundred pound shaved ape chasing him around the apartment.

As if there weren't enough oddities with Reesie already, it wasn't long before we noticed something else. One day we watched Reesie walk casually across the floor while sporadically thrusting his hips. We didn't know what was going on, so we kept an eye on him. Then he did it again. And again. We were worried that it might be something to do with his deformed rear legs. But once he tried to jump on Sparky's back, which Sparky violently protested, we realized his legs worked fine, as did his hormones. The dog had begun to hump everything: Sparky, the toys, the couch, my leg (teaching him to "be a bear" just encouraged him), a pillow, even the air. When he walked, he'd break out into these lower-body thrusts while his head looked around like he didn't even know what he was doing. Disco music played in my mind every time he walked by, which was funny until he attached to my leg. Allyson and I agreed that it was time for Reesie to get neutered.

We took him to the same folks that neutered Sparky: same price, same procedures. We'd drop him off in the morning and wait to pick him up at about five o'clock. Except this time they called us around noon. The tech seemed surprised when she told Allyson, "This is unusual, but Reesie's already up and eating and ready to go home." When we got him just after lunchtime, he was wide-awake and seemed nearly unfazed. He was so unlike Sparky, who acted like he'd been hit by a truck after the procedure. Reesie's behavior was more like *Well, look at that…my nuts are gone! What's for dinner?*

Despite his quick recovery, the disco music still played as he continued to hump his way from one place to another. The vet told us that it might continue for a little while, but he'd plane out eventually. In the meantime, we just had to let things run their course.

****

Allyson and I lived in several apartment complexes while in Dallas, and never really took the time to get to know our neighbors. We were friendly to each other and carried on great conversations from time to time, but didn't develop many long-term relationships. Apartments seemed to be transitional to the people who lived there anyway. Many of the occupants were single parents, college students, or new families needing a place to stay while they scoped out their future dream homes.

We didn't have many things to move; so when the rent went up at our complex, we'd often move to a different and more affordable one. Since owning Sparky, we moved to new complex on the second floor just like the previous. Though we preferred a first-floor apartment, they seemed to be in highest demand, so it was pretty tough to get one.

At the new complex, Allyson struck up a friendship with a young college student. Her name was Nichole, a petite brunette studying to be an architect. Even though she was one of the hoity-toity first floor residents, we didn't hold a grudge. Well, not much of one, but we did tease her some about her good fortune, all of which she took in good stride. She was generally quiet and polite, but knew how to have fun. We both liked her a great deal and invited her over from time to time for dinner or to watch a movie. She too was a dog lover but didn't have any pets at the apartment. Sparky and Reesie loved seeing her and became her—as she put it—"doggie fix" to get her through the days when she missed having her own dog. That worked out fine for us, especially when Allyson and I went out of town and needed a dog sitter.

Although she was single, we didn't expect someone as great as Nichole could stay that way for long, and we were right. Allyson ran into her at the mailbox one day when Nichole mentioned that she had been out on a date with a guy she met at work. She was smitten already. His name was David. He and his parents had moved from somewhere in Europe several years ago. It was all dark and mysterious, something that drew Nichole to him all the more.

That evening when she told me the news, Allyson said that she wanted to invite Nichole and David over for dinner and to play a few card games. I thought it was a great idea, especially since we were both fond of Nichole and wanted to see if this David guy was up to par. Plus, we were simply curious about how the tall, dark European would look. Allyson and I envisioned a Rico Suave; we'd have to see it ourselves. Allyson called and set the date and we got everything ready for our game night.

****

Three knocks sent the dogs into their usual fury. Once we calmed them down, Allyson and I opened the door together so that we could both get a preview of Rico, I mean David. There was Nichole wearing makeup and a generous dose of perfume, her hair frozen in place with hairspray. She glowed as she introduced David.

David had a modest stature, standing with great posture only a few inches taller than Nichole's small figure. He had a medium build, and seemed to be in good shape. His skin wasn't as dark as we thought it would be, in fact he seemed almost as pasty as I was. Though he was balding on top, his hair was dark and just long enough to fit into the small ponytail he had tied up in the back. That was the edgiest part about him; everything else fit a conservative mold, including his pleasant, almost business-like demeanor.

At dinner we got to know him more. He was talkative, funny, and interesting, and Nichole's eyes glistened at every word he spoke. It was clear that David was tall, dark, and handsome enough for her. On occasion, Allyson and I glanced at each other with an approving nod. David really was great despite our false presumptions about his looks. In fact, he was better than we imagined. The Rico Suave image we presumed made us feel like he was a player who was uninterested in a real, long-term relationship. In reality David seemed like a keeper.

We finished dinner and moved to the living room where we talked some more. Later, we played a few games of Gin Rummy on the floor, feeling that it would be more comfortable than playing at the table. Each of us rested our backs against the bases of the couch, love seat, or ottoman, depending on where we sat. I was never any good at Rummy and it didn't look like David was either. The girls clobbered us over and over, and they rubbed our noises in it with flirtatious delight. Despite our mutual defeat, David and I still got along great.

Everyone was having a good time, even the dogs. Sparky occasionally nudged one of his toys over to someone's hand to get a toss. We finally told him to stop, and he sat next to Allyson and chewed on his honking Mo-Mo the rest of the night. Reesie had already circled the dinner table a dozen times looking for any crumb of food and finally came to join us on the floor. Since David was the new guy, Reesie thought that he was the most interesting person there. At first he was shy about meeting David, leaning in carefully to sniff his hand and then fleeing when David reached to pet him. But after about twenty minutes Reesie lay on his back next to David letting him rub his belly. When David stopped to play a hand in the game, Reesie nudged David's hand with his nose so that he'd keep rubbing. We all got a kick out of it.

"That's enough, Reesie," I said, and called him over to my side. He stayed there for a few minutes, but soon the restless pup wandered off again, got a drink of water, and came back to the living room with his long tail wagging. We were all engrossed in the game when Reesie jumped up on the couch that David rested his back against. I noticed him there when he began eagerly sniffing the back of David's head. Allyson noticed too and gave me a strong *this-isn't-good* look.

Before I could react, Reesie had mounted David's head biting down on the lone tuft of hair atop his balding dome, and humped faster than I'd ever seen, the ponytail frizzing at every thrust. I was frozen in shock for a second or two, cheap disco music playing in my mind.

"Oh…hey! Whattaya doin' back there?" David asked, showing a hint of surprise. I had to hand it to the guy, even though the rest of us completely freaked out, he stayed cool the whole time. I grabbed Reesie, but the crazy dog wouldn't stop jostling and refused to release his grip on the mouthful of hair. I had to pry his teeth apart with my fingers before the music finally came to an awkward halt.

The night just kind of ended after that. Nichole said that they needed to be going. I couldn't imagine why. Allyson and I apologized profusely as Reesie's tail continued to wag, but there was no recovering dignity after our dog's little show. Nichole and David left, I closed the door and sat down on the couch with Allyson, saying, "Well, we'll never see them again."

And we didn't, at least not like we used to. Allyson saw Nichole only a few times in passing, but Nichole never had the time to talk. She moved out not long after that anyway, so we liked to believe that she just became engrossed in her time with David and maybe even married him. But we knew the real reason.

Honestly, it's hard to get over someone screwing with your head.

THEY ARE PICKY EATERS

It may have been the commercials I saw growing up showing petite dogs eating velvety gourmet dog food out of crystal dishes that fed my stereotype about them being picky eaters. But my time around Sparky and Reesie suggested different tastes.

The early morning studies at my desk contributed to my new vision of a dog's diet. The New Testament tale about the rich man and the destitute pauper, Lazarus, described wild dogs regularly licking the diseased pustules all over Lazarus's body. It made me gag just thinking about it. An Old Testament proverb stated that a dummy that keeps making mistakes was like a dog that keeps trying to eat his own vomit. My own dogs had already demonstrated that nastiness. In the Bible, dogs consumed a lot of disgusting things, including human blood and corpses. Reading some of these accounts, I swallowed hard over my morning coffee and cherry danish.*

Allyson and I paid more attention to the dogs' diet anyway, especially since Reesie needed to lose his gut. The vet's warning that his weight could lead to back troubles and paralysis caught our attention. So we made sure to measure out his meals carefully, and to take him outside as much as possible. The apartments we lived in at the time had a community walking track just a stone's throw behind it, which worked out beautifully for us. Allyson and I used it several times to exercise, and thought that it would be good to take the dogs around it once. So late one summer afternoon, we leashed them up and started for the track.

When it came to walking on a leash, Sparky was a natural. He'd trot happily in front of us in the middle of the sidewalk, always staying ahead of Reesie to make his alpha-dog position clear. That was no problem for Reesie, who spent most of his time catching new scents off the sidewalk. He'd stop, smell the same spot for a few seconds, then try to lead us another direction. We'd call him back with a little tug on the leash to keep him walking our way. He came to know what we expected on a walk, but couldn't shake the desire to blaze his own trail. On this particular journey around the walking track, we wanted him to get good exercise, so we didn't stop moving.

The paved serpentine track was in an open field of lush grass curving its way around trees and gullies. A gorgeous park like this must have been irrigated well in the middle of Dallas's hot and dry climate. The summer heat could easily kill the vegetation, especially if there was a drought. As a swimming pool serviceman, I knew just how hot it could get, and I wondered how well our dogs would take it. But we made it a point to go about an hour before sunset to take the edge off the heat. Still, even the low temperatures could be a stifling ninety-five degrees that time of year. But really, how bad could this one walk be?

Sparky did well. Allyson and I were convinced that he could make it a few more times around the track. And if we had brought a tennis ball to motivate him, we'd wear out before he would. His trim, athletic physique impressed everyone he trotted past. His thin coat probably kept him cooler, too.

As for Reesie, the poor dog was in dire straits. He was already slower than Sparky, and weighed more than him too. About halfway around the track he got slower. He insisted on sniffing out points of interest longer, but we kept tugging him along. His normal panting became excessive with his tongue hanging out of the side of his mouth. Allyson and I decided to give him a break for a little while as we talked about his situation. He plopped on the ground in the shade and panted away. The dog needed to exercise, but maybe this was a bit much. We wondered if we should just carry him back. Still, he was a young dog and could probably make it back without any help. One of us thought he should give it a try. I think it was Allyson's idea.

We made it maybe another fifty feet when we decided to carry him back the rest of the way. Seeing his bowed rear legs begin to tremble is what did me in, that and thinking about how his thick black coat probably made him twice as hot as Sparky. We rested a few more minutes, gave the dogs some water from the bottle Allyson carried, and made our way back with Reesie in my arms. When we got home, the water bowl became Reesie's best friend. Normally, he'd get some water then come sit in one of our laps, but not this time. He drank some water then lay down on the cool linoleum floor in the kitchen next to the bowl. When he cooled off, he finally visited us in the living room. Allyson lay on the floor beside him and gently stroked his back.

"Sorry, Reesie," she told him. "We've learned our lesson. You'll get shorter walks from now on."

We never took the dogs on the track again, though we did take Sparky to the field next to it to throw his ball every now and then. Instead, we walked them closer to our apartment so that we could quickly return when one of them tired out. We also tended to let Reesie lead us on his on his own when he caught a scent. We felt we owed that to him since we almost gave him heatstroke.

It was on these little scent trails that we started to witness Reesie's peculiar tastes. He'd galumph along the edge of the sidewalk until he caught an odor, took a few quick breaths, and led us off the grass on a hunt. Sometimes it would lead nowhere and he'd stop and look around bewildered until we got back to the sidewalk again. Other times, he'd find something interesting. By "interesting" I mean something really gross like a half-eaten chicken bone, an old greasy hamburger wrapper, a decomposing squirrel corpse, a dried up earth worm; you get the idea. The first couple of times Reesie found these things I let him approach and sniff, until I realized that he didn't want to sniff, he wanted to consume. He'd get a taste and I'd pull him back in disgust.

"Reesie! What the heck, man! That's disgusting!" I'd say. If Allyson was with us, she'd break out into gagging, "*Whulp! Whuuullllp!*" It may have been the thought that Reesie tried to lick us both in the face as often as he could. Now that we knew the remnants of a dirty diaper might be stuck to his teeth, it didn't seem as cute.

It was gross, but it sort of reminded me about my dad's dog, Moes. He may have eaten everything he could find, but I still believed Reesie was a very smart dog. For example, Reesie began to understand that I'd pull him away from anything gross he found before he could eat it. I'd let him sniff, but that was all. So he compensated by forgoing all sniffing; once he found it, he instantly ate it. And if he couldn't swallow it before I pulled back on the leash, he'd grab and eat it as I tugged and generally freaked out, usually with Allyson gagging in the background.

No matter how big it was, Reesie could eat it:

A French fry. *Omnom, gulp!*

A pizza crust. *Omnomnom, gulp!*

A donut. Omnomnomnom, gulp!

A dead bird. Omnomnomnomnom, gulp!

The "dead bird" thing really grossed me out. That actually happened when Reesie was off the leash. The apartment buildings encircled a garden area where we could let Sparky and Reesie out to go potty. Of course, Allyson or I would be out with them to keep an eye on things. That day it was just me. Sparky had found something that interested him and was rolling in it. Reesie was intrigued and went over to investigate. That's when I noticed his head bobbing up and down. As I walked closer, I saw Reesie nibbling at this mess that resembled the remains of a bird. About ten feet away I froze and ordered Reesie to stop. His teeth still embedded in the feathers, he froze and looked at me.

"That's right. Let it go!" I ordered. Eating discarded food was one thing, but a dead bird was probably loaded with bugs and parasites which could mean more vet bills.

Reesie actually listened. He released the bird as his head raised.

"Good boy!" I said and took a step forward, and Reesie quickly bit down on the bird again and froze, staring right at me.

"Don't you do it! You'd better let that thing go!" I said. But he continued to chew despite my threats. I made a run for it, and he grabbed the bloody mess and took off, eating and running at the same time.

I finally caught him and said, "Oh no you don't," sticking my finger in his mouth and down his throat to salvage what I could. He didn't bite me, but he resisted with everything he had. By the time it was over, I had a fistful of feathers and guts in my hand. I winced, partly because I knew that Reesie had eaten half the bird already and partly at realizing there was a squished bird in my hand. I don't think that he got sick from that incident, but I almost did. And you can bet that Allyson replied with more than one gag when I told her the tale.

Reesie's determination to eat all things rancid was a mystery to me particularly because of the look on his face while he chewed. He'd furl his lip at every putrid entrée as if to say, "This is horrible. I must have more!" Even pain didn't dilute the dog's love for food. While Sparky didn't really care about anything after being neutered, Reesie couldn't get enough kibble right after surgery. Eating was apparently how Reesie coped with pain. Nothing illustrated that better than the Hot-Dog Incident of 2004.

I got home from work before Allyson did that day and let the dogs out into the courtyard to do their business. I was throwing the ball with Sparky when I noticed that Reesie was missing, no doubt on one of his quests. That's when I saw his tail sticking out of a cluster of holly bushes. I called to him, but he didn't come. When I walked up and pulled back the bushes, I gasped at what I saw. Someone had thrown half of a hot dog onto an ant bed, and Reesie was fighting the ants for it. He stood at the edge of the dirt bed chewing while a thousand ants climbed up his legs and along the hot dog onto his snout.

"Let it go, you dumb dog!" I yelled, frantically dusting the ants off of his face. But it was hard to reach him since he and the shimmering ant bed were between two prickly bushes. Though he was squirming, he didn't give an inch. The lunatic was determined to eat that hot dog before the ants could finish eating him. As I dusted him off, the ants started biting me, too. Unable to reach him completely, I dusted and twitched while he ate and twitched. Now desperate, I took a different approach pulling out of the bushes, grabbing his waist from behind, and dragging him out. As he emerged, I noticed that he gulped down the rest of the hot dog. Mission accomplished. I dusted the rest of the ants off both of us, got us all inside, and gave Reesie a bath to make sure all the ants were gone. He was amazingly resilient to the ant bites, a trait I envied as I noticed several of my own sizable welts rising on my hands. He had the advantage of a thick fur coat that the ants couldn't penetrate right away. I sort of wished I had something like that to protect me; it even would have helped keep the holly leaves from scratching me.

At the end of it all, I thought about how Reesie would fare in one of those commercials for fancy dog food. I was sure he would eat whatever they put in front of him, whether it was in a sparkling crystal bowl or buried in the middle of a glistening ant bed.

THEY WON'T TAKE PILLS

Giving medicine to the dogs was…well, a pill. The first few years that we had Sparky and Reesie, the vet occasionally needed us to give them medicine for something like worms or stomach problems. If we were lucky, the pills would be small, but for some reason they usually seemed even larger than pills a human might take. Naturally, we had to break those up into halves, which made things worse in a way since then we had to give twice the number of pills. We did our best to come up with creative ways to get them down their gullets.

At first we started with the basic method: sticking it down the throat and praying that the pill didn't come back up. A little research on the Internet said that you could put it down a dog's throat, hold the snout closed and stroke the throat until they swallowed. I read one that said you could blow lightly in their faces, which would also help them get it down. Maybe that worked well on the bigger dogs, but our small dogs usually found a way to spit the pills out. So at the end of it, we had slobber all over our hands, a slimy pill slathered with spit on the floor, and a dog that wouldn't open his mouth for you again.

Another website suggested that we could go to the kitchen and just casually drop a piece of lunchmeat on the floor and the dogs would eat it instantly. Then, we could drop the pill and they'd eat it before they knew what it was. The first part of that procedure worked fine, but the second part didn't. A piece of ham or turkey would rarely reach the floor before a dog ate it.

But when I dropped the pill, they lunged at it, examined it, and summarily rejected it. Another method, please!

Wrapping it in lunchmeat or cheese was one of the more effective methods. They'd happily gobble it up, but we'd occasionally find a white glob on the floor, which turned out to be a regurgitated pill. It absolutely blew my mind that Reesie would regularly eat as much garbage and refuse that he could find outside, but couldn't bring himself to eat a simple pill when he needed it the most.

So, we considered another method found online, one that required mashing the pills into a powder and mixing it with something like yogurt. But that seemed to be a lot of work to give a pill two or three times a day. There had to be a better, more efficient way to get it done. More than once I wished out-loud that all dog pills were the easy, chewable kind like the heart-worm cubes we gave them once a month. The dogs were so happy to eat those they'd nearly swallow the cubes whole without a single chew. The irony was funny and frustrating.

The most effective method came from our memory of Bill the Breeder himself: peanut butter. If we hid the pill in a generous gob of peanut butter, the dogs would eat whatever we'd give them. In fact, they'd both fight to get to the pills so much that they'd almost bite our fingers. It was just the kind of eagerness we needed to make sure they actually swallowed the pills. Though Allyson was nervous that it would make the dogs pudgy, it didn't affect them at all. I suppose Reesie didn't get much exercise when he was a pup, but now our walking regimen had his stomach smaller than ever. I suppose the fact that he was maturing and growing longer helped hide his weight well, too.

Even though we both gave the dogs their pills when prescribed, I ended up doing it most of the time. Part of the reason was that it just fit in with my routine: get up, let the dogs out, feed the dogs (give pills), sit at desk, study for class. Since I gave the pills in the morning, I often gave them in the evening too out of routine, but I'd forget sometimes. So I tried to align the dogs' pill schedule with my own. I had an assortment that I took in the mornings and evenings, which included vitamins, supplements, and allergy medicines. If I was sick, I just added the prescribed pills to my routine. When the dogs needed medicine, I'd give them theirs at the same time I took mine.

For convenience' sake I carried all my own pills in a single ziplock bag that I kept in my computer satchel. It was a lot better than carrying them around in their own bottles. I had tried that before, but all of the pills rattling around the containers annoyed me and everyone nearby. It was the worst when I walked into a class during a lecture. Students could hear my pills shaking as I approached, rattling as I opened the door, and jangling all the way to a desk in the middle of the room.

Yeah, the pills in a ziplock bag made everyone happy.

One evening, Allyson and I were reading in the living room when I realized it was "pill time" for me and the dogs. To assemble the troops I called both of the dogs with my usual happy tone: "Ya'll ready to take your medicine?" Sparky showed up right away, ready to gobble up whatever peanut-buttered capsules I gave him. But Reesie didn't show.

That was odd for a few reasons. Allyson and I had found that Dachshunds had to be near their owners at all times. That is, unless they are into trouble. Reesie could either be hiding because he knew he had done something he shouldn't have or worse, he was doing it right now.

"This can't be good," Allyson said. "We'd better go find him." She went to one side of the apartment while I scoped out the other, which happened to be the extra bedroom I used as my study.

I approached the doorway and called him, "Reesie? Where are you? Are you into trouble?" I listened but didn't hear a sound. I turned on the light and called again. Nothing. I made my way around the bed to my desk at the other end of the room and found my computer bag open, the contents strewn on the ground. I knew better than that. I should have put it in the closet like I always did, but must have forgotten this time. The first thing I saw was one of my books pulled to the middle of the floor. It was a beautifully bound, very expensive reference book that I bought just a week earlier. Three of the corners had been chewed off completely, its value and beauty marred forever.

"REEEEESIEEEEE! I'm going to kill you, you stupid freakin' dog! Where the heck are you?"

Reesie had chewed on things before, and I usually took it well. But this just sent me over the edge. I knew it was just a book, but it was one that I prized more than any of the others. I sat quietly in my chair until I heard something a few seconds after my outburst.

Thump, thump, thump, thump....

It was the sound of Reesie's nervous tail pounding the floor, and it came from under the bed. I lunged to the floor to seek him out.

"There you are you freak of nature! Come here so I can…!" and then I saw it. My ziplock bag of pills was torn open, pills strewn on the floor, and some of them had been chewed. Just then, Allyson showed up. "What happened?" she asked.

My head popped up from behind the bed and I said, "Reesie's gotten into my bag, and I think he's eaten some of my pills."

"Oh no!" she said. "Which ones?"

"I don't know. The bag was torn open and they're all over. He chewed on some, but I don't know how many. He may have eaten some, or none. What do we do?"

I tried calling Reesie out so that we could look him over, but he didn't trust me, probably because I sounded like I was going to eat him alive just a minute before. He came to Ally, though, and we looked him over. We noticed he had a powder all around his mouth, so he must have eaten at least one of the cold medicine capsules. Reesie was in trouble.

Allyson called her sister Heather who worked for years as a certified vet tech. The phone was on speaker so we all could talk. After Allyson told her what happened, Heather suggested that we induce vomiting by giving him a capful of hydrogen peroxide.

"Is that safe?" Allyson asked.

"Yes, it's fine," Heather said, "as long as it's not past its expiration date. It will fizz in his stomach to make him throw up. That way you can look at what he's eaten and see how serious things are."

I tore into the bathroom, grabbed the peroxide, and thundered back in a flash. "Just a capful," Allyson insisted. I nodded and sat down next to Reesie on the tile floor at our front door entrance. I poured out the cap and offered it to the dog, who looked shaken and peculiar. It could have been the pills, but it might have been his reaction to my crazed sprints around the house. He lapped up the capful and we waited. After a minute, nothing happened.

"Give him another one," Heather said. We did and again, nothing. Reesie's tail wagged at every dose. Apparently he was enjoying the new effervescent drink.

"That's crazy!" Heather said. "Most dogs his size would have vomited by now. Give him one more."

At the third dose, Reesie stood immobile as a statue. His tail stopped wagging, instead pointing straight behind him, and his stomach groaned. "Here it comes," Allyson said. And it did, over and over again. Reesie started heaving and finally gagged up a foamy mess, and to both of our surprise each gob was fluorescent orange. Allyson, the more medically minded of us felt around the foamy piles but couldn't locate the remnants of any pill or capsule.

"What is this orange stuff?" she asked. "Are any of your pills orange, Jason?"

"No. What the heck has he gotten into?" I said.

"Was there only a bag of pills under the bed? Was there anything else?" Allyson asked.

133

I ran into the bedroom, hit the floor next to the bed, and pulled everything out. He had dragged several things under there, but one was a wrapper that was different from bag of pills. I pulled it out and read the label: "Cheese Crackers with Peanut Butter."

"That's what it is!" I yelled. "He ate the snack crackers out of my bag. Maybe he didn't eat the pills at all."

Heather interjected, "You can't know that for sure unless you take him to the vet. If you think there is any possibility he took a pill that could be harmful, you really should take him. But it's up to you. You could wait it out and see how he responds."

Ally and I looked at each other and nodded. Allyson said, "I think we'll get him checked out just in case. Thanks, Heather. We've gotta go!"

"Okay. Tell me what happens. Good luck!" Heather replied and hung up. We were out of the door in less than a minute, on our way to the emergency vet. We didn't even worry about pinning Sparky up, because he was already hiding under the other bed, probably afraid we'd give him peroxide too. Since I already had Reesie in my arms, Allyson drove. The fact that she drove faster than me didn't hurt, either.

On the way there, I could feel Reesie's heart rate and breathing grow faster. We had no way of knowing what was causing it. He hated riding in the car anyway, because it often meant that he was on his way to the vet; and he was right this time. It could have been Allyson's driving, which was faster than usual and made me even more anxious. But I feared the worst, that it was one of my pills working its way into his system. I agonized over wanting to help him but didn't know what else to do. My eyes teared up at the thought that I might lose him on the way to the vet.

"I've killed my dog, Allyson! I can't believe it! I may have killed him!" I went on and on like this most of the way there.

"Don't talk like that! We're almost there," she said, swerving from lane to lane.

"Don't die on me, you freakin' stupid dog!" I choked and pulled him close. "You can eat the rest of my book when we get home. Just don't die!" He tried to lay his head down, but I shook him awake. I didn't know if he was trying to sleep or die.

Just as Allyson promised, we pulled up to the vet clinic a moment later. When we got inside, they took Reesie back right away and checked him out. Allyson and I waited in the lobby for what seemed like forever when someone finally came out to give us an update.

It was the vet himself who said, "Reesie seems to be doing fine. We're inducing more vomiting and so far, so good; but I do have a question for you. Has he eaten anything orange recently? All we're getting is orange foam. I understand the foam comes from the peroxide you gave him, but what about the orange color?"

We told him about the peanut butter crackers and he laughed, "Okay, that explains it. For the life of me, I couldn't figure out what that was."

"Is he gonna be okay, Doc?" I said, a little embarrassed.

"Yes, he should be fine. He doesn't show any signs of toxicity. If he did eat anything poisonous, it looks like we got it out in time. You were smart to give him the peroxide. Now we'll just wait until his stomach calms down, give him some charcoal to absorb anything we missed and he should be ready to go."

When he left, we had to wait about another half-hour before Reesie was ready. At one point, I stepped back outside for a breath of air. The clinic was in a strip mall. Though some of the windows were blacked out, I could see through some parts. Lo and behold, there was an exhausted Reesie on a table in front of a tray of mushy orange gunk. I was glad to see him alive, but I could tell the poor dog had had enough for one evening.

Once we were ready to go, we paid the steep emergency clinic bill and headed for home. Reesie's face was wet with peroxide, vomit, disinfectant, and who knows what else; but he was also ready to sleep like a rock on the way home. After that night, I took extra steps to make sure all my medicines were put away when I got home, because I knew it would either cost me a dog or a huge vet bill if I didn't. I also started to realize just how close I was getting to these silly dogs. I could see why Chuck could tear up just talking about giving up his German Shepherd. Maybe shedding tears over losing a pet didn't show that a man had a weak spine. Maybe it meant he had a big heart. Maybe the stupid dog in my lap was helping my own heart to grow.

THREE IS TOO MANY

At school and my morning studies, I found that the Bible had a lot to say about children and parenthood. One of the more poetic references is in Psalm 127, which calls children a gift from God and relates them to arrows that a warrior would carry into battle when one faces his enemy at a city's entrance. I always found it peculiar when people quoted this passage to thank God for their kids, since it treated children like ammunition instead of flesh and blood, praising their usefulness instead of their innate value.

Allyson and I never seriously talked about kids the first few years we were married, preferring instead to spend our time enjoying each other. Before long we noticed that our peers and friends were having kids like crazy; my classmates talked about their kids regularly as did Allyson's coworkers. Allyson had landed a great job as an occupational therapist and was doing very well. Though money was still lean, we weren't in terrible shape, which helped us start thinking about having a baby.

Though we had an itch for kids, Allyson and I never really had an overwhelming desire to have any. I know I didn't. I didn't even know how to hold a baby the right way. One day Allyson and I visited one of our friends in the hospital who just had a baby of her own. She and her husband were happy that we came and asked me if I wanted to hold their son. I said no, but they insisted. Again, I said no. I'm sure I looked awkward when they handed him to me anyway. I don't know what it was exactly, but I always felt like I might

137

break or drop a baby, which was probably why I looked like a buffoon at that moment. I'm told this is a common experience for guys, but that day I must have had *FAIL* written all over me. The nurse in the room came over and said, "Oh sweetie, let's try this again. Let me show you how to do that."

She was only trying to help, but I felt pretty dumb about it all. She repositioned the gurgling bundle of joy correctly in my arms, which was supposed to be more comfortable for both the baby and me. But I wasn't since I thought moving out of that posture would get me another crash course in baby-holding methods from the nurse.

After a few minutes in a frozen state with an awkward smile on my face, Allyson came to my rescue and took the little tyke from me. Unlike me, she was a natural with kids, so she cradled and gently rocked him while easily chatting with the happy couple. As we left, we passed by the nurse's station where we overheard a nurse talking about the dude in room 204 who didn't even know how to hold a baby the right way.

Even though I'd have to learn how to handle a kid eventually—I'm told nobody is really prepared to—I was willing to start our adventure in parenthood. We figured the dogs would also be good around kids since they had both matured. Reesie wasn't humping every-thing around him anymore, which reduced the risk of his sporadic copulation with our baby's head or diaper bag. We'd just have to make sure he was never alone with the baby or baby supplies, or else we'd find him eating formula powder, lotion, or dirty diapers. Sparky would be cool, as long as the baby didn't grab his tail.

Ally and I tried to get pregnant, but after several visits to doctors and specialists, we discovered that having our own kids just wasn't in the cards for us. There were other methods we could try, but we were not prepared for them at the moment. Adoption was a possibility too, but that would be an expensive and lengthy process that we weren't ready for. We had to face that fact that we might never have kids of our own, which was a tough pill to swallow no matter how much peanut butter was involved. Allyson and I held each other closer than usual those days. Even the dogs could sense something was wrong and were both constantly at our sides. About two weeks later we were back to normal, or so I thought.

It was a weekday around 5 p.m. when Allyson called me. She was heading home from work while I was wrapping up my own day.

"Hey Hon! What's up?" I said.

"Oh, nothing. Just heading back home," she said. Her tone was a little more syrupy than usual. It got that way when she was going to ask for something. "You know, I've been doing some thinking…."

"Uh oh, that's not good," I said. "What exactly have you been thinking about?"

"I want another dog."

I was silent. *Another* dog? How can she want *another* one?

She continued, "So we've decided that we're not going to have kids, which saves us a ton of money, and I have wanted a girl dog since we got married. We're not having kids, so I want to do this."

"Hmm…."

I tried to say *no*, but this came out instead. Allyson knew that two dogs was already pushing it with me. One was enough, two took getting used to, but three would be insane. More dog food to buy. More poop to scoop. More sporadic vomiting and attempts to eat it. More telling the dogs to be quiet when they barked at car alarms, talking neighbors, and buzzing flies. More vet bills. The only plus I could foresee was that we now lived on a first floor apartment, so we wouldn't have to worry about carrying dogs up and down an endless set of stairs. But the negatives outweighed the positives, so I gave my final answer.

"Okay. We'll start looking."

Did I just say that? Yes, I think I did.

Despite all the potential negatives, the truth was that Allyson had always wanted a girl dog. And since we were still reeling over the fact we weren't having kids of our own, a new addition might be a good thing. So when I got home that evening, I found Allyson on the Internet scoping out Dachshund breeders. She had already decided on a name, too: Dixie. All that was left was to find a dog befitting the name.

Since our two dogs came from different homes, we decided to get the third from a different place, too. Allyson found a ranch that bred Dachshunds, so we made the appointment and headed out to the country one afternoon. The ranch was beautiful and spacious. The owners were an older married couple that came out front to meet us as we pulled into their long driveway. We talked a bit about what we were looking for as we made our way inside.

The outside of the home was a rustic log cabin, hiding a more luxurious interior. We made our way down the hall to a separate wing connected to their large home. It was like a guest home with it's own separate rooms and kitchen. The couple remodeled this section as their own Dachshund quarters; the original walls between the kitchen and den were removed to make a single circular room where the dogs had plenty of space to play, though they weren't there at the moment.

The old couple asked us to sit in the middle of the circular room, where they introduced us to one lone, red Dachshund. She was the mom to the other pups we heard yipping in another room. She was a beautiful strawberry blonde, with short, soft fur, long ears, and a sweet disposition. Once she sniffed Allyson's hand, she approached and locked eyes with her for as long as Allyson looked back, happily accepting all the rubs Allyson gave her. When I said hello, she broke her gaze with tilted head and positioned herself in front of me. She sniffed my hand cautiously, approached so that I could rub her neck, and stared straight in my eyes too. It was a gentle but intense stare, as if she was examining us as potential parents for her kids. She became comfortable with us, climbing up into our laps, but always gazing—almost smiling.

"She loves to stare, doesn't she?" Allyson asked as she stroked the mamma-dog's back.

The lady replied, "Sure does. She's done that since she was a baby, but even more since we bred her. She's a very sweet dog, and her pups have always been the same way. Ya'll ready to see 'em?"

"Absolutely!" Allyson said. "We're ready when you are!"

A few moments later, the unmistakable sound of stampeding wiener pups reverberated down the short hall into the circular room. Five tiny Dachshunds rummaged in, headed straight for their momma. They were hungry, and that's all it took for mamma to break her stare and run for her life around us in the circular room with her pups in hot but clumsy pursuit.

"We're weanin' the pups, but they still aren't there yet," said the breeder with her country drawl. The weenies continued to circle us in a hilarious chase.

Once they calmed down we got a better look at them all. Some were bigger than others, but they were all covered with a thin red fur, suggesting that they'd be just like their momma. They were playful too, chewing on each other's ears and rolling around on the floor giving yips of joy. We asked about prices as we greeted each one. Though Allyson and I were enamored, we were still looking for a good deal.

"We can work out a good price," the lady told us, "don't you worry 'bout that. I like a good profit, same as the next gal. But I'd rather the dogs get a good home. Why don't ya' tell me about your dogs some."

As sure as the momma-dog was sizing us up, the breeder lady did the same by asking us good questions about how we treated our dogs. We were impressed at that kind of screening, which was something the breeder didn't have to do. It showed that she cared about the dogs more than the money she could get for them, especially since she said she had refused to sell to some people because they didn't seem responsible enough. But our stories convinced her that we were okay. All that was left was choosing the right dog.

All five pups were great, but one was particularly interesting. "Why is this one priced lower than the others?" I asked.

"Take a look at her tail," the lady said. Allyson picked up the female and saw the bend in the middle. It was about a 45° angle in the center of her tail pointing it down.

"Oh my goodness!" Allyson said. "How did it get like that?"

"It's a defect. Sometimes it gets bent in the womb. When they're born, their tails are still soft, so you can try to straighten it out some. We did as much as we could, but that's about as straight as it'll get. It'll be fine all her life, but if ya don't like it, you can get it lobbed off."

There was something pretty cute about how that crooked tail wagged. It was dark at the tip too, resembling an oil dipstick. The pup held it up high so that it wouldn't touch the ground as it fanned back and forth. Like her mom, she just stared at us and wagged, and if we didn't get to playing with her right away, she'd try to jump-start us with a few yips. She wanted us to get involved with what she was doing. And somehow, Allyson thought these were all the qualities that a dog named Dixie should have. So that was the dog we chose.

A FEMALE WON'T BE DIFFERENT

We already knew that Dixie shared some key traits with her mom—the staring and the red fur, for example—but we started seeing her own distinct personality right away. The most noticeable trait was her daintiness, a "southern belle" quality befitting her name. She was a cute puppy who grew into a beautiful dog. Every time we took pictures of her, she'd notice and look directly at us before the camera clicked. Those who saw her pictures talked about how photogenic she was and that she looked as if she actually posed for her photos. I had a suspicion that she did, especially since she used her beauty and winsomeness to get what she wanted all of the time. It beguiled us more than once.

When she grew to full size Dixie was the shortest of the three dogs, but her body was about the same 15 to 18 pounds as theirs. Her shorter stature may have had something to do with the fact that her head was so small. Her body grew as long and plump as a wiener dog's should, but her head, ears, and snout were smaller than the others. Her neck was the right size, but there was no difference between the size of it and her head, which made taking her for a walk tough. If she found something that she wanted to chase, she'd give her head a little twist to pop her head out of the collar and off she'd go. Even though she had stumpy legs, that didn't make her slow by any means. When I

144

shouted for her to come back, she'd turn and see me—
this giant ogre yelling and chasing at her with a crazed
look and swinging leash—and she'd just run faster. If I
tried tightening the collar to keep it on, it would be
way too tight for her to breathe. I couldn't do that to
the dog; and if I did, I was sure to hear about it from
Allyson. After a lot of trial-and-error, we decided a
shoulder harness was the best way to keep Dixie under
control.

I use the term *control* loosely, because Dixie was
completely unpredictable. When Allyson and I used to
walk Sparky and Reesie, we each got a single dog to
manage which always made for a relaxing walk.
Sparky moved straight ahead while Reesie stayed
close to the grass to see what treats he could find.
Once we included Dixie to the routine, everything
changed. The biggest difference was how Dixie
thought she should walk with us. We would all go
straight, while she darted left, right, backwards and
forwards, often tying all of our leashes and legs into a
confusing knot. If we approached a streetlight, she
circled it twice before we passed. On one of these
walks, Allyson gave Dixie the nickname *Dee-Dee*. But
I thought her zigzagged trots required a better name:
ADD.

While she winded around every post, mailbox, and
sign in sight, she just might eat whatever was in front
of her before Reesie got it, which turned the two dogs
into furry self-propelled vacuum cleaners roaming
from side to side down the street. Luckily, Sparky
didn't care as much about eating everything he found.
He was the alpha dog on patrol engrossed completely
in the walk. Part of the alpha's job description is to

stay on point in front of the pack, so it really ticked him off if anyone got ahead of him. All three dogs were on retractable leashes, and one might get right beside Sparky from time to time. Sparky pulled as hard as he could on that leash so that he could get ahead of his oblivious opponent once again, wheezing and coughing as he choked himself on the collar. He had to be in the lead; that's just the way it was.

Walking them all at once meant that one person was responsible for two dogs while the other had only one, and that person ran poop patrol. It's what I called the job of picking up after the dogs with plastic bags. For the record, I did it most of the time. To her credit Allyson tried more than once, but when she felt the warm mush of freshly dropped poo in the plastic bag along with a whiff of the moist, ripe odor, she didn't handle it well: "*Whuuuullp!*" Then a muffled gag. Swallow. "*Whuuuuullllp!*"

You get the idea. To my recollection she never vomited, though I expected it with the full-body convulsions that accompanied her gags. The noise often got the dogs' attentions. Dixie would run from us and hopefully not pop out of her collar, Sparky would start to tremble at about a category 5, and Reesie waited eagerly for what Allyson might produce. I was very tender about it all, at her side the whole time laughing my head off. She would do her best to reply, "SHUT UUULLLLP!" And I'd fall out laughing all the more. She'd wipe her mouth, I'd wipe the tears from my eyes, she'd hand me the tepid bag and yank the extra leash from my hand, and that was that. No more poop patrol for Allyson.

That scenario played out a few times until I just assumed bagging the brown mush from then on. It's a good thing, too. I can only imagine what our nutty troop looked like to someone walking down the street. A trembling, wheezing dog leading an extra-long black dog chewing on something that died two days ago, followed by a zigzagging dog with a freakishly small head wrapping her leash around her humans: a convulsing, gagging lady and her crazy husband cackling like a lunatic and waving around a mushy, bright blue bag of poop. Who wouldn't want to get to know them?

Sometimes the dogs would find something to roll in, but Dixie was hesitant to join. Don't get me wrong, she liked to roll in something stinky as much as the next dog, but she had refined tastes. Something had to smell especially interesting for her to throw herself in it. And she frequently found an odor that was just too foul to tolerate, which meant it had to be buried right away—not with her paws, but with her nose. On occasion we'd see her elegantly scooping dirt or leaves on top of the offense, which periodically drew Reesie's interest. If it was too foul for Dixie to tolerate, it was likely a perfect snack for him.

That's not to say that Dixie had no disgusting tastes. If it didn't have a horrible odor, she would at least give it a taste. It was only a matter of time before we discovered her favorite outdoor treat. Funny thing is that we discovered it while we were all *inside*. Allyson found a slimy strip of…something on the kitchen floor one day and couldn't identify it. It wasn't moving; it was just sitting there being gross. She cleaned it up, but found another a few days later. It turned out that Dixie liked to chew on old, dried up earthworms she'd find on the sidewalk. She'd hide one inside her mouth until she got home and then got to chewing on it. When it became too soggy, she'd abandon it in the most inconvenient place possible, like in front of the TV or in the seat of the recliner. Her smuggling operations worked until we finally caught on. One day we found her trying to abandon one of the gooey worms again in the middle of the kitchen floor. When I scolded her, she bowed her head in penitence and tried to cover the mess with her nose. There was that cute thing again, screwing up all my correctional guidance.

Speaking of correctional guidance, Dixie was the worst at potty training or any other kind of training for that matter. Without question, she was the most stubborn of our three dogs, and I think she knew it, too. If she snuck away to poop in another room, she'd come back to where Allyson and I sat and began barking excitedly while giving us that patented Dixie-stare. The first time it happened, it had an urgency that sounded like, *Timmy's fallen in the well!* But actually it was, *I took a dump in the bedroom and you need to clean that crap up!*

Now, her barking could have been Dixie's way of blaming another dog for the crime; but when I found the pile, I knew for certain it was hers because it had her own signature. For some reason, she didn't see any need to stop moving while going potty. She would strut around like Groucho Marx until she was finished, scattering her logs about in an abstract pattern in whichever room she chose to display her masterpiece.

It was the cutest way to befoul a room I had ever seen, and she was always proud of her work.

Furthermore, that dog was the canine urination champion of the world. Though she was smaller than the other two dogs, she easily peed more than both of them combined. It must have had something to do with the veritable gallons of water she drank throughout the day. If she couldn't eat whenever she wanted, she'd drink…a lot. So much so that we had her checked out by the vet, but he cleared her of any ailments. I suppose she just liked drinking, which meant she had to go outside more than usual or she'd take care of it herself in the apartment somewhere.

That was extremely frustrating to me, especially since her peeing only encouraged the other dogs to have their way in the house, too. One day, I caught her just after she finished. When she saw me, she did what she normally did and rolled over on her back in submission. "Dixie!" I yelled, then took a deep breath and shook my head. I got down on my knees and elbows so I could be nose-to-nose with her and looked her sternly in the eyes.

"You know better than that, you little runt," I said.

Her eyes were wide. She looked worried and licked the end of my nose.

"You know you're not supposed to pee in the house," I said, trying to keep composure.

She licked me again.

"Stop it, Doofus! I'm serious. You've gotta knock this crap off!"

She stayed frozen, thought about it for a few seconds, then reached one of her munchkin paws up and placed it lightly over my mouth and licked my nose again until I grinned. It was the stubborn and cute combination that made this southern belle of a dog so hard to handle.

If Dixie thought she was in any kind of trouble, she would roll on her back just like that. So, she rolled over quite a bit. Among the three Dachshunds, It was easy to spot the guilty party of any crime. If I pointed to something eaten, or chewed, or pooped on and Dixie was guilty, then she'd roll over while the other dogs wagged their tails, not knowing what was going on. You might think that it meant she was sorry, but that's not it at all. She'd roll over with her tail wagging. At times, the tail would freeze, which I think signified true regret.

But she wasn't all surrender. If Allyson was petting Sparky on the floor, Dixie would charge in at full speed, force her way between Allyson's hand and Sparky, and roll over for a belly rub. She felt like she needed to be the center of attention. She'd wedge that tiny head anywhere if it would get her what she wanted.

Her hunger for attention probably motivated her barking, too. If she ever wanted food, or to go outside, or to have her stomach rubbed, she'd give the Dixie-stare and start with the barking. It was cute at first but quickly became an annoyance, especially if Allyson and I were relaxing in the evening. On the other hand, her constant adoration when we came home from work every day made us smile every time. She wouldn't just bark, she barked and howled in a truly unique way. Her howls were like words, as if she was trying to tell us all about her day. She wouldn't stop until we got down on the floor to see her; it was flattering for sure.

Dixie might have been annoying at times, but it was hard to shun her when she did so much to get us to notice her every day.

Dixie wanted everyone to love her, and she had our hearts pretty quickly. Even Reesie fell for her, and she adored him. She used his soft, fluffy stomach as a pillow whenever she fell asleep. We owned a basket with a pillow inside it for a dog to use as a bed. When Reesie jumped in it, Dixie had to be there too, even though it was designed for one dog at a time. When Reesie was on the couch, Dixie had to be next to him at all times. If she couldn't be beside him, she'd lie on top of him, and Reesie didn't mind at all. The biggest gesture of love was around the food dishes, where Reesie would actually allow Dixie to eat from his bowl. If we ever needed to take Reesie to the vet, Dixie was a wreck. She'd whine persistently with wilted ears until he came back, and once he did she'd sniff and bite him playfully all over, howling out her long and happy conversations.

She loved Sparky too, but he didn't take to her right away. The alpha dog of the Garrison pack needed time to accept our new addition. He saw her as more of an annoyance at first, especially when she tried to take food from his dish, or if she took his toys, or if she tried to lie on top of him. Any attempts to move into his territory or personal space led to a lot of growling. Dixie got the message and stayed clear of him most of the time, but she never gave up. After a few months, Sparky started sharing things with her. The real breakthrough was when they began playing together with Sparky's toys and Sparky allowed— even encouraged—Dixie to play with his Mo-Mo.

When they skipped around the house chasing each other, the Mo-Mo honking at every step, we knew that she had finally captured Sparky's heart, too.

SHE'S EITHER A CHICKEN OR A SHAR PEI

It was Dixie's constant desire for love and acceptance that made her roll onto her back. Anytime we had guests the first year we owned her, she'd meet new people happily. She was a little skittish at first; but after a couple of sniffs, she would roll over and let her new friends rub her stomach. After that, she'd be confident enough to push Reesie and Sparky out of the way to get that person's attention. Each guest also got plenty of the Dixie-stare for good measure, meaning that they were all right in her book. She was very friendly like that, so we didn't think anything about introducing her to some of the neighborhood children.

Sometimes Allyson and I would take two of the dogs for a routine walk and then let the third go on a special outing where we could turn them loose without a leash. It was Dixie's lucky day, so we took her out to a grassy area where we could let her romp a little. As I insinuated before, she was shorter than the other two but had a thicker, more sausage-like torso that limited her flexibility, which may have been why her run looked more like a rabbit hopping than a dog running. Allyson and I always got a kick out of seeing the little frankfurter flop across a field.

Even funnier was the first time we noticed that her back legs sometimes ran a different direction than those in front. It made her run straight toward her destination with her torso at an angle. Her long body was like a fire truck with front and rear steering; but it seemed the rear guiding mechanism was a little off, steering a little too far left or right. She always got to where she needed to go, but she wasn't efficient at it.

On the other hand, the way she always started all of her sprints showed more panache than any of the other dogs, especially if she wanted to run to us. After all, we could best see it if she was coming straight toward us, or sideways toward us (depending on the angle of her body). First, she'd freeze and give Allyson or me the Dixie-stare. In an instant, she'd decide to sprint and—this would all happen in half a second—her front legs hopped straight up then her back legs propelled her forward.

Essentially her first step was a dramatic pounce of crazy joy, and then she'd scurry over to us and immediately roll on her back ready to receive a belly rub, all while her crooked tail wagged wildly. That beginning pounce always made me think of the Lone Ranger's popular shout, "Hi yo, Silver! Away!" I heard it in my mind every time she ran.

A few elementary-aged girls were out playing nearby when they heard us laughing and throwing a toy with Dixie. I overheard one of them say "Hey look! It's a weenie dog!" which had them both blazing a trail toward us. They ran up and cordially asked if they could meet our dog, and we were delighted to oblige these two young ladies.

"Sit down and take a second for her to meet you," Allyson said with a smile. The girls plopped down and jutted their hands toward Dixie, no doubt wanting to see who would be the first to pet her. Dixie recoiled at their quick moves.

Allyson stroked her back and told the girls, "Slow down. Be easy. She doesn't know you yet." Both girls held their hands out at the same time. Dixie carefully approached, sniffed, stared, and rolled over. Chock up two more friends for the southern belle.

After a few seconds, one of them took Dixie's stuffed toy and began to play with her. The girls took turns tossing the toy and Dixie would retrieve it, crooked tail wagging. They had such a great time, they stood up and moved out into the field for more room. Allyson and I enjoyed watching them play. The girls laughing and Dixie prancing, it was as if we had two girls of our own playing with the family dog.

Just then, three boys about the same age as the girls showed up. While the boys were several yards off, one of the girls waved at them. Then I heard the boys shout something and charge toward the girls at full speed. That's when Allyson and I thought that we might need to go over and collect Dixie, but one of us insisted that things were okay. I can't remember who it was—probably Allyson.

Wanting to get a closer look at Dixie, the boys crowded around her, all petting her at the same time. Dixie hunkered down, her crooked tail touching her stomach, and her tiny head jerking several directions wondering who these new giants were. The girls tried to tell the boys to back off, but the boys weren't listening. Dixie saw an opening and—*Hi yo, Silver!*— fled the group with such speed that her rear legs almost outran her front. The boys laughed and chased her. One of them took her stuffed toy and threw it next to her—or at her, maybe.

"Stop!" I said, approaching the group. The five kids got quiet and gave me an innocent look. I was amazed at how quickly they produced it. "Just what the heck are you guys doing?" I asked.

"We were just playing with the dog," one of the boys said.

"Did you ask to play with her?"

"No, they didn't!" said a girl. "They just came up and started messin' with her!"

"Nuh-uh! We didn't do nuthin wrong!" yelled another boy.

"Well, Dixie is *my* dog," I said. "I was watching you all the whole time, and you boys came on *way* too strong. You scared her to death. I mean, she was running from you guys and you chased her down!"

"You have to be gentle with a small dog like this one," Allyson said. "You'll scare her otherwise." She had just arrived with Dixie in her arms. She had to coax Dixie out of a hiding spot in some bushes. The kids apologized and asked to pet Dixie one more time. Allyson held her while the kids stroked her one at a time. Dixie was trembling. She didn't trust any of them.

Even though they were just being kids, that encounter changed Dixie from that time forward. It could be that she was just nervous by nature anyway, but we think that the boys at least amplified the problem. Anytime she met new people, either at home or outside, she'd hide behind Allyson's or my legs. She'd watch how the other two dogs reacted before she made a move of friendship, and even then it could take about an hour before she approached the visitor on her own. The best way to introduce her to folks was the method we used with the two girls. We still use that method today.

Dixie's nervous nature showed up in other ways. If she heard something outside, she'd bark to get Sparky and Reesie's attention, then retreat behind them. Inside, she'd hear a noise at the door, let out a few barks to alert the other two, and then retreat as they advanced to investigate. Allyson called her our little chicken. I laughed, "You may be right!"

But there was that one day I thought of her more as another kind of animal. I still cleaned swimming pools at the time, and one of my customers owned two peculiar dogs that I'd never seen before. They were much bigger than mine, probably close to one hundred pounds each. They each had a wide snout, short ears, and a thick curved tail, which touched the top of their lower backs. But the most distinguishing characteristic was their thick, loose skin. They looked like they had too much of it, especially around their faces and necks where folds of skin almost hid their eyes and ears completely. They weren't the friendliest of dogs (not sure if that had anything to do with the breed), but the male let me pet him a few times.

The fur was prickly and the skin rolled around at each stroke. After a few moments, I could feel a growl emanate from his chest and thought that would be enough for the day. Their presence was intimidating, and I often wondered if they would attack. The swimming pool could be an escape, but I didn't know if they could swim.

When I got home, I researched these strange, loose-skinned mongrels to find out a little more. I had good reason to be wary of them since these Chinese

Shar Peis were originally bred as hunting and (later) fighting dogs. The websites I visited noted that loose skin was helpful in fending off attackers that try to grab it. It made sense to me as I remembered how much the skin rolled around in my own hands. While I found the dogs intriguing, I've never thought about owning one. The fact that the two I knew always felt like growling at me when I visited their home made it clear to me that wiener dogs would do just fine, at least for now.

As was prone to happen at times, I got home from work before Allyson one summer afternoon and took the dogs for a walk. Taking all three of them together was impossible, so I took Sparky and Reesie together first, then Dixie by herself. It was a normal walk for them all, with an occasional stop here or the eating of something disgusting there. It was too early for their dinner, so I made myself a tall glass of ice water, sat on the couch, and turned on the TV. Sparky and Reesie jumped on the couch with me, but Dixie was out of sight and started to whine. *She must be in the kitchen asking for dinner already*, I thought.

"Quiet, Dixie! It's too early," I said.

It got quiet, and I heard her lapping up some water. She whined again. I ignored her. She lapped up some more water, and whined after a few seconds. Again, I ignored her. It was not unusual for her to whine that much. The plump little Ballpark Frank liked to eat and regularly complained to get dinner early. What *was* peculiar was the amount of water she was drinking. Lapping at the dish over and over again was not like her, so I decided to check things out.

The first thing I noticed as I turned the corner was the amount water on the floor around the water bowl. It was much more than usual. What I mean is that Dixie was the sloppiest drinker I had ever seen. Her lapping splashed water everywhere and she'd normally dribble some out of her mouth as she walked away. Sometimes I wondered if she plunged her wee head in the bowl and sloshed it around until water somehow found its way into her mouth. She got everything wet when she drank, but there was much more water on the floor than usual this time.

I turned the corner into the kitchen and found Dixie. She was standing at attention, crooked tail aflutter, and half of her face was swollen and sopping wet.

"Oh my God! Dixie!"

"Mwuph!" was her muffled reply.

I knelt down and examined her face, supposing that something bit or stung her on the nose and I just didn't notice it before. When I touched her snout, she whined and wiggled free from my grip. I called Allyson right after that. She was always my go-to on things like this because she worked in the medical field. I wasn't sure if veterinary medicine coincided with occupational therapy at all, but I figured she had to know more about this than I did.

She answered. "Hey, babe. What's up?"

I got right to the point: "Dixie is swelling up like a balloon!"

"What? What happened?"

"I don't know. I just took her for a walk and now half her face is swollen up!" I heard Dixie lapping up more water. I called to her and she looked at me.

Water poured out of her mouth. Her whole face was puffy now. The skin was swelling up around her eyes and closing them up in giant wrinkles. "Dixie's a Shar Pei! We have a Shar Pei!"

"What? What are you talking about?"

"She's swelling up! What should I do?"

Allyson's cooler head prevailed. She said, "You have got to take her to the vet right now. The closest one is just around the corner next to the bakery. Go right now, and I'll meet you there."

I didn't bother putting up the other two dogs. Sparky was under the bed anyway, probably trembling at a category 6. Reesie was lapping up the water off the floor. Neither one of them was swelling, so I grabbed the miniature Shar Pei and ran to the car.

By the time I arrived at the vet clinic, the swelling had worked it's way down her neck and something like goose bumps had progressed down her back, so they treated her immediately. Allyson showed up soon after, asking all sorts of questions that I really didn't want to talk about. The vet concluded that it was an allergic reaction of some sort and that it could have killed her if we left it untreated. Ultimately the swelling would have choked her, so it was a good thing that we brought her in. That day we also learned that Dachshunds were more prone to such reactions than other dogs. Lucky us.

"Mwuph!" was what we heard when we saw Dixie again; her crooked tail fanned so hard we thought it would fly off. The swelling had gone down some, but they still created wrinkles around her eyes. Allyson took one look and finally understood my Shar Pei rambling an hour earlier. We had to watch her closely when we took her home that night. The medicine we gave her had her pacing and whining for several hours. More frustrating was when she started swelling up again that same night. We called the vet and had to take her back for another injection, which meant more pacing and more whining. Though Dachshunds are prone to these reactions, apparently Dixie was ultra-prone. Again, lucky us.

It wasn't until morning that the swelling finally subsided completely. We kept the other two away from Dixie while she was on the mend. That morning, we put them all together again where they sniffed and playfully clawed at each other. Before we left for work that morning, we put the dogs in the kitchen and set up the gate. Sparky barked us out as usual, but the long night had taken its toll on Dixie. She was already lying against Reesie's stomach sound asleep.

HE CAN'T REACH IT

While finishing up my master's degree, I began looking for places to continue my studies. Allyson and I both recognized that if I wanted to go into education, a doctorate would be a great advantage especially if I ever wanted to teach in college. Dallas offered several great opportunities for education, but was more than a ten hour drive from my family, and much more than that from Allyson's who now lived in Florida. And for all Dallas's splendor, Allyson and I missed the culture of southeast America. After all, I grew up there and Allyson did for most of her life, too.

After looking for several months, we found a school in Memphis, Tennessee that was closer to home and offered a degree with the kind of concentration I wanted. Though I wasn't ready to dive right in as soon as I arrived, I was confident I'd be accepted into the program. After some soul searching, we decided to go ahead and move there right after graduation. I planned on taking a year or two off before starting school, giving me a break from studies that Allyson and I both could use.

I got a job teaching English and Religion at a private school, which started a few weeks after I finished my classwork in Dallas. For the last few years, Allyson had been working for one of the most prestigious hospitals in Dallas, so finding a job in Memphis was no problem for her. In fact, one center asked her to come out right away, so we moved her and all of our things (including the dogs) into an apartment in Memphis; but I came right back to Dallas and stayed in school housing until I finished my last summer term. We were apart for only about six weeks, but it was pretty rough to be away from her that long. I can't imagine what it's like for couples that work in different cities.

The last day of school, I packed everything into my pickup early that morning, turned in my room key to housing, and went to class. When it was over, I said my goodbyes, hopped into my truck and headed east on I-30. Knowing that I was just hours away from seeing Allyson was a terrific feeling. And I had to admit, I really missed seeing my dogs, too.

The drive to Memphis took about six hours, and I indulged in each one. Of course, I was thrilled to see Allyson and the dogs again, but also basked in the joy of completing my last master's level class. Since I had already missed summer graduation, I'd have to decide if I wanted to go to the January ceremony. But what was more important was the fact that I was DONE! I was also eager to start a new job as a teacher in a few weeks, a step up that got me away from cleaning pools under the sweltering Dallas sun. Earning a living in an air-conditioned environment was more than a little appealing.

While musing over these things, the sun began to set behind me. By the time I reached Memphis, it was totally dark. Only the streetlights on the freeway and my headlights gave any illumination. Eventually I found my exit, which would take me to my new apartment just outside of the city. The road led me through miles of complete darkness amid pitch-black fields of corn and cotton. The only light on the road came from my own headlights, a stark difference from

Dallas's resplendent streets. I rolled down the windows and relished in the cool night air—another thing that we didn't much of in Dallas, especially in July. Overjoyed, I hung my arm out of the window and let out a howl. I was just minutes away from my new home and my misplaced family.

The streetlights came into view again as I reached my suburb. I found my apartment, parked in the familiar lot, and made my way to the front door with a bag in each hand. Allyson met me outside, wrapped me up in a fabulous hug, and covered me with kisses.

"You're home!" she said. "For good!"

I almost pulled a smile-muscle when I said, "I KNOW!" and squeezed her even tighter. "And I'm done with school!"

"I KNOW!"

More kisses.

The three weenies went ballistic just behind the door when they heard my voice. When I went inside, Sparky and Reesie clawed at my leg for attention while Dixie ran circles around me belting out a tirade of barks and howls, filling me in on all I had missed since my last visit. She finally got in front of me and showed her teeth, a kind of smile she shared when she got excited. In the face of such glee, I had to get on my stomach to greet them properly, which created a mosh pit of clawing, rolling, and piling all over my head and back. I think one of them peed on me some, too.

After they calmed down, Allyson helped me bring in the rest of my luggage. When finished, I walked into the living room and found Sparky perched atop of the couch backrest, something he did regularly. Still aching for my attention, he wagged his tail and leaned his nose toward me. Any further and he'd fall to the floor.

"Take it easy, Sparky," I said, walking over to him to give him a rubdown. A few seconds later, Dixie charged up there, too. I was surprised she could manage it with her stubby legs. Then Reesie wanted to get in on the action, but he wasn't as nimble as the other two. Jump after feeble jump, his bowed legs just couldn't manage.

"Reesie, you don't need to get up here," I said. "Your back legs are too weird for that."

Determined to prove me wrong, he continued to hop up from the seat of the couch, but his strange rear legs just couldn't perform. Then he moved to the arm of the couch and tried jumping from there.

"Reesie, sweetheart," Allyson said, "you're too clumsy to get up there. You're better off on the ground." That was the truth. Sparky was the most athletic of the three; Reesie was the least. His unusually long, lanky body combined with his misshapen legs was a bad combination for a would-be couch climber. But so he wouldn't feel left out, Allyson pulled him up to the top of the couch herself, holding him stable so that he wouldn't fall. Those few minutes holding all three dogs chest high with Allyson at my side allowed for a nostalgic family hug, the perfect welcome-home gift.

****

Our new place was another two-bedroom, second-story apartment beautifully set in front of a lake and several pine trees. It drew a number of ducks and geese, which Sparky loved to ogle and chase every chance he got. If it weren't for the leash, I was sure he'd catch one. Then again, I don't think he'd know what to do when he approached it. The ducks would run, but the geese stood their ground, hostile even to humans who casually walked by. I doubted that Sparky would stand a chance. As for Dixie, she'd give a few barks and run the opposite direction. It was that way with pretty much everything she encountered. Reesie the explorer was indifferent. He preferred searching for some kind of rotting treasure to gobble up rather than accosting a family of birds. When I took two dogs out together, I learned that Reesie should be one of them; because when Sparky charged the birds and Dixie ran from them, it made for terrible walks.

After a few months, Memphis began to feel like home. Allyson was a great occupational therapist, and a perfect fit in her clinic. Her coworkers found the techniques that she learned in Dallas invaluable. As for me, I had never taught in middle or high school before, which proved to be the toughest job I ever had. My degree prepared me for higher education, research, and church work, which I thought would be a great fit in a religious-based private school. And it was, but I didn't anticipate all the other responsibilities demanded of a secondary teacher. I didn't know how all the other teachers did it without breaking a sweat, while I could barely keep up. I came home late most nights, ate dinner, and got right back to work grading papers. Though I lived for the weekends, I spent most of them working as well.

Balancing the stress and workload was almost unbearable that first semester, but my principal was sympathetic. More than once he found me working late in my classroom and demanded that I stop everything and go home. He could tell that I was having a tough time adjusting and told me that many first-year teachers struggle, but if I could make it to Christmas Break then things would become more manageable the rest of the school year.

Despite his encouragement, I wasn't sure I could do the job much longer. By the end of October, I wasn't sleeping well and a routine visit to the doctor revealed elevated blood pressure. I was cracking up. I wondered how the heck the other teachers reached a level of performance that I just couldn't attain. Everyone told me I was doing the right things, but I was still buried. Christmas Break couldn't come soon enough.

Lucky for me, Fall Break came before that; so Allyson and I planned a getaway to the deep woods of Gatlinburg Tennessee. We had our honeymoon there years ago, so it was a great time to relax and reminisce. It was also a time to leave all my work behind and decompress. We left the dogs with a friend of ours and hit the road. The trip was fantastic, and luckily the dogs didn't cause any trouble for our dog-sitting neighbor. We returned late Sunday evening, collected our dogs and went home. Allyson and I needed to get into bed since we had work the next morning.

I didn't sleep well that night. The time in Gatlinburg made me feel like a normal person again, but the thought of going back to work already had me stressed. After tossing and turning in bed all night, I got up at 5 a.m. for my routine morning study where I could to go over my lessons for the week. I fed the dogs, took them out, and sat at my desk with a cup of coffee and a box of Dunkin' Donut glazed donut holes we got on the way home from Gatlinburg. These were the very best donut holes from my favorite donut company. Since Memphis didn't have a Dunkin' Donuts at the time, I cherished each hole as I soaked it in coffee and ate it nice and slow.

At 6 a.m., I needed to get ready for work. So, I turned off my desk lamp and walked out of the room. But the dogs didn't follow me as they usually did. Instead I saw them sniffing around the desk, trying to find a way to climb up and get a few donut holes for themselves. Reesie was balanced on his back legs "being a bear" sniffing around the edge of the desk and licking his jowls.

"Just what the heck do you think you're doing?" I said. "Those came from halfway across the state and belong to me. Don't get any ideas."

They all gave me the penitent dog look—wilted ears, head bowed, tail tucked—as if to promise that they would never even dream of touching dad's prized culinary possession. I wasn't convinced, so I rolled the chair away from the desk as a precaution. Now there was no way in the world they could get up there. I turned off the lights and made for my morning shower.

I had just toweled off when I found Sparky and Dixie in our short hallway looking mortified. It reminded me of an ancient story I studied in school, the Gilgamesh Epic, where a flood so terrible frightened even the Mesopotamian gods, who cowered against a wall "like dogs."* Apparently, ancient dogs hunkered too, and here I saw the perfect image of that scene as two of my own groveled against the wall with their tails tucked and an expression that screamed "We promise! We didn't do it!"

"Hey you two," I said. I was friendly, but perplexed. "Where's Reesie?" Sparky's tremors registered a category 6 and Dixie wouldn't even look at me. Instead, she rolled over on her back in absolute surrender. Just then I heard a familiar sound coming from the study. *Bap! Bap! Bap!*

I tiptoed into the dark room; my eye twitching a little at what I saw. My precious donut box lay on the floor turned on its side. The front half of Reesie's body was deep inside it. Only his rear was visible with his long tail contently wagging its full range of motion, pounding out a happy rhythm on the now empty box.

I erupted like a volcano. "REEEEESIEEEEE!" His tail froze. He slowly backed out of the box, faced me, and sat down. Crumbs of the now lost pastries peppered his black face. Though he knew he was caught red-pawed, he still had the audacity to lick the frosting from his nose. It was silent for a few seconds as I glared at him until I heard the faint *tap! tap! tap!* of his tail. Only the very tip eked out an irregular rhythm that sounded like a dirge. I heard another noise too. It was the faint sound of Sparky's jowls smacking as he just achieved category 7.

I was furious. I learned a long time ago that the best action to take in that case was no action at all, or else I'd do something I'd regret. I took a few deep breaths until the moment passed. Allyson's arrival helped change my mood.

"Good grief! What happened?" she asked, rubbing her squinted eyes. My shout woke her, and probably the neighbors, too. When I told her what happened she wasn't very sympathetic: "Geez, take it easy Conan! They're just donuts!"

She was right, of course. But it wasn't just the donuts. It was the combination of the stress at work, lack of sleep, and the fact that I thought I had secured the room. But even a little wiener dog could outwit my strategies, leaving me feeling incompetent and insecure. I could really use a donut.

Crap.

When I looked back at Reesie, my glare had faded into apish confusion. "How the heck…? I pulled the chair back from the desk. There was no possible way for you get up there. No way in the world!"

"Looks like he found a way. He's pretty persistent when he wants something," Allyson said, and sat down next to Reesie to cuddle him. After a few more minutes, the other dogs came out of hiding and joined in. "Looks like Reesie can do more than we thought!"

Once I stopped seeing red, my eyes opened wide at the peculiar revelation. With an awkward body and deformed legs, Reesie was the least likely of the dogs to reach those donuts. But somehow, he did it. The other dogs fled, but he stayed. His desire and work brought him to a level he'd never achieved before, and the rewards were sweet. That is, until I came into the room and considered selling him to a sausage factory. It was an odd lesson in determination that I took to heart. Maybe my own breakthrough was just around the corner, too. Without even trying, Reesie had given me a second wind and reminded me that even the impossible might be achieved if I didn't give up. Wearing a new smile, I joined everyone on the floor for a little playing.

Reesie's unintended lesson helped me make it to Christmas Break and ultimately four years at that school. I finished the first year strong, and the subsequent years even stronger. Those years of teaching were some of the most rewarding of my life.

THEY AREN'T INTERESTED IN CLOTHES

Nice as the apartment was, our plan was to live there only for a year while we searched for a house. We had dreamed about our first home since we were married; but because we were new to Memphis, living in an apartment gave us the chance to get to know the area before we committed to a mortgage. Since Memphis was much smaller than Dallas, it was a slower lifestyle with less stress. While Dallas was *go-go-go!* Memphis had a more easy-going feel, which made it simpler to get to know people.

As soon as we moved in, we met our neighbors upstairs. They were two guys in their twenties who went to college together, but had just graduated and started their careers. We also got to know the lady across the hall, and the family downstairs. It made our block the friendliest we had experienced since we were married.

The guys upstairs were the best help. Though they didn't have any pets of their own, they both loved dogs and were happy to help dog-sit when Allyson and I needed to get away for a weekend. Occasionally we got together for cookouts, game nights, and movies, too. Before long, we thought of them more like younger brothers than neighbors.

We became so fond of them, Allyson decided to set one of the guys up with Mallory, a friend from work, and it was a hit. Smitten on the first date, they got into a serious relationship with a promising future. Allyson was pretty happy with the results, now seeing herself as an accomplished matchmaker. Mallory was so elated, she called one day to ask if she could come by and drop off a token of her appreciation. Allyson agreed and before long there was a knock at the door. Mallory walked in with a big smile and a gift bag with yellow tissue paper pouring out of the top.

"It's just a little thank-you gift," she told Allyson. "Actually, it's for one of your dogs. When I saw it, I just had to get it. Go ahead and open it!"

When Allyson pulled out the tissue paper, her eyes grew wide. "Oh my goodness! That is *so* cute!" She pulled out a simple fluorescent pink cloth. At first I didn't understand what it was, but when I did I slapped my forehead.

Mallory was a fellow dog lover who owned a female Chihuahua that she often dressed in fancy clothes or accessories. It seemed that her dog Stella had a full assortment of these outfits. No matter where she went, Stella wore something fashionable, even if it was just a bow on her head or a tiny bandana around her neck. So once Allyson held up the pink cloth and showed me the shoulder straps, I realized that this was a dress for dogs. Technically, it was a pink tank dress.

"I love it! Jason, look," Allyson said.

I was very positive. Really. I smiled with my hand in my hair, saying, "Oh boy. Mallory, that's great but you really shouldn't have."

She knew it irked me, which made her and Allyson laugh all the more. "As soon as I saw it," Mallory said, "I thought it would be perfect for Dixie!"

"It is. Let's try it on!" Allyson said. All the dogs were already circling our feet wondering why we weren't giving them the attention they deserved. Within seconds, Dixie sported a skin-tight, hot pink, tank dress that shamelessly showed all her curves, bulges, and folds. The girls howled with delight.

"She loves it!" Mallory said as Dixie ran around the room, her wagging tail a blur behind her. Allyson agreed and insisted that I look, too. I covered my face in shame, but did get some glimpses when I peeked between my fingers. Dixie's photogenic nature and southern belle personality worked perfectly with the bright pink threads. And I had to face it, she loved all the extra attention she was getting. Still, I couldn't be one of those people who dressed his dog up all the time. But as the night moved on, I got a kick out of seeing Dixie enjoy the attention. It was also funny how Sparky seemed interested, too. He ran around with Dixie sniffing and biting at the dress.

I decided to let the girls talk and moved into the living room so that I could watch some TV. Suddenly, I heard Allyson and Mallory laughing again. I just ignored it and kept watching the news. I didn't notice how quiet it got until Sparky pranced around the corner, a fuzzy ball in his mouth and bright pink dress covering his body.

"Aw, COME ON!" I shouted. The girls roared with laugher again.

Mallory stopped long enough to say, "Looks like he likes dresses, too!" She and Allyson kept laughing as Sparky continued to wag his tail. I supposed as the alpha dog, he had once again become the center of attention, which made his day.

"What are you doin' to me, you two?" I said. "I'm having a hard enough time with Dixie wearing a dress. But Sparky too?" The giggles continued as I peeled the clothes off the proud little wiener dog. "That's great. Our alpha dog is a transvestite. Does that even work if dog's don't wear clothes?"

The girls couldn't answer because both were rolling with laugher. Luckily the dress was too small for Reesie, otherwise he'd be part of our little fashion show, too. Needless to say, I was glad when the night was over.

A few weeks later, Allyson was getting ready for work when she gave me some exciting news.

"Take a look at the sides of Sparky's face," she said.

"Okay, what am I looking for?" I asked.

"I added some color to his cheeks."

I blinked and asked, "Excuse me, what? Did you say you're putting makeup on our dog? Our male dog?"

"Yeah, he wanted me to! He was standing on his back legs trying to reach me while I put on my blush, so I gave him some. I think he liked it!"

"Well, I'm sure the other dogs would have acted the same way."

"I tried to put some on them, but they didn't care. Only Sparky wanted it, and boy he couldn't get enough!"

I slumped a little and looked as Sparky, "Now you want to wear makeup? What's up with you, dude?" Sparky, who can get a little strange when he gets excited, couldn't find a ball to chew on; so adding insult to my ego's injury he decided to mount Reesie's back while Reesie obliviously chewed on his own nails. I sighed, then said, "Sparky, knock it off." He climbed down and looked for a ball to chew on instead. Just then, Reesie's head jerked left and right: *What just happened?*

I threw my hands up and said, "Well, all right. Our dog is gay."

Allyson laughed and tried to reason with me. "He's not gay, he's just excited."

"Yeah," I said, "excited about dresses, makeup, and showing Reesie some love. You know, he could have tried that with Dixie, but didn't. Let's keep an eye on him when he wanders around the house. He might come out of our closet wearing your shoes one day."

I was just joking. Sort of. I knew that Sparky had to maintain his status as the head of our three dogs, but did he really have to do that by making the strongest fashion statement? I also thought the thing with Reesie was another alpha task, but this time he was wearing make up.

Frustrated, I looked at Sparky again and said, "You're a dog! Eat the clothes, don't wear them!" Dixie must have overheard me, because she decided to do just that.

Before moving to Memphis, a friend from work sold me his bedroom set, which included a new queen sized bed. We certainly enjoyed the extra room, as did

Sparky who still found annoying ways to spread out as much as possible in bed every night. The other two dogs were in a spacious, collapsible kennel that could house a Great Dane if necessary. It was plenty of room for them at night, and Sparky joined them while we were gone during the day. Getting them all in there didn't take much. Simply saying "You wanna go in the kennel?" had Dixie and Reesie inside waiting for a treat before I could reach the last word. Sparky took a little more convincing, but he couldn't overcome the draw of a moist liver treat.

Our new bed was also roomier underneath, which gave all the dogs a nice hideout when it was bath time. That was fine, because it also had more room between the frame and floor, so we could now reach much farther underneath if we needed to grab a dog hiding there before bath time. Of course, if that was still a problem, the dreaded broom was always available to sweep them out. But more than a hiding place, it became a stash for all sorts of Dixie's finds.

I became suspicious something was going on while I was in the shower one day and saw a red blur scurry past the glass shower door. When I asked Allyson about it later that morning, she claimed she had seen it, too. We didn't think much of it until Dixie walked up to Allyson one day with something on the end of her nose. It was a piece of some wrapper that she salvaged from the bathroom trash.

"And just where did you get that, Dee-Dee?" Allyson asked. She wondered if the dog had eaten the whole thing, but after looking around a little we found the stash. A heap of wrappers, receipts, socks, and more than anything else, pairs of Allyson's underwear chewed to shreds.

"Dixie Garrison! Bad dog!" Allyson scolded. "So this is where all my underwear has been going?"

Predictably, Dixie rolled over on her back in total surrender, but that wagging crooked tail and glint in her eye said she regretted nothing. When we weren't looking, she continued raiding the bathroom trash can and clothes hamper. The thieving little blur was so sneaky at it, we didn't even know her smuggling operations had grown from earthworms to…well, everything made of paper and cloth. Obviously, she preferred to eat women's clothing instead of wear it. I think it hurt Sparky's feelings.

So we took steps to ensure she couldn't nab any more goodies. Clothes had to go immediately into the hamper, and the lid had to be replaced. We got a new trashcan with a lid to take care of the wrappers and kept an eye on things we left on tables since Dixie could find a way up there, too. Despite all the effort, Dixie still found a way to smuggle her goods under the bed, taking advantage of any moment we might be preoccupied.

One evening I came home and greeted Allyson with a nice long hug and she wouldn't let go. This could mean one of three things. As a therapist, she might have just returned from a continuing education course where she learned a new pressure point that she wanted to find on me. If I suddenly felt a pinch followed by a headache and an urgent need to urinate, then that was probably what she was doing. It could be that she was sad and just wanted a nice long hug. In that case, it would be noble for me just to hug and do nothing else. Boring, but noble. Luckily it was the third option. The mood hit us both just the right way, so the hug continued and the kissing began. The dogs sensed all the excitement and began barking and jumping at us both. We laughed at their jealousy and kept right on going. To me, the dogs didn't sound jealous. Instead I heard, "Go Dad, go!"

It was a fantastic evening, if I do say so myself, that involved a new lacy outfit (Allyson's, not mine). After the festivities, I noticed that the outfit was missing.

"Uh oh," I muttered and looked under the bed. During times like these, the dogs usually retreated to the bomb shelter under the bed frame and waited until the sirens stopped and the rumbling ceased. So it was no surprise when I saw three sets of glowing eyes gazing back at me. One set turned counterclockwise; it was Dixie rolling on her back again.

"Aw, Crap! What do you have down there, Dixie-dog?" I said.

"She'd better not have my new lingerie," Allyson said.

Without a word I salvaged a pile of treasures and placed them on the bed one item at a time beside Allyson's knee: a wrapper, a sock, the remnants of a cardboard toilet paper cylinder, and a mound of shredded red cloth that used to be a dainty, sexy outfit.

Allyson just shook her head. "I just bought those. We've got to be more careful when she's in the room."

I climbed onto bed and mused, "Well, at least Sparky wasn't wearing them."

Allyson chuckled, "Are you sure? Maybe he's the one who dragged them down there."

My lip curled as I looked at the ceiling, "That's not an image I want to think about right now."

THE OTHERS ARE IMMUNE

Our searching had finally paid off. Nearly a month before our lease was up at the apartment, Allyson and I bought our first house. It was a humble starter home in a beautiful suburb just outside of Memphis, a three-bedroom single-floor home with an attached garage on a zero-lot line. We were both thrilled about this big life step.

We had a few weeks left at our apartment before we had to move out, which gave us time to make the changes we wanted in the house before we moved in. The previous owners had a dog that did a number on the floors and carpets, so we had the carpets replaced and some of the floors fixed. During summer vacation, I didn't have to teach so could devote every day to getting the house ready for our move-in day, painting and patching wherever needed. I cleaned every square inch of that house relentlessly. When everything was ready inside, I focused on the outside. The back and front yards were overgrown, so I borrowed a lawn-mower for the initial cut until I could purchase one of my own. The back yard was only a few hundred square feet, but since it now belonged to Allyson and I, it felt like a thousand acres in the middle of no-where. A seven-foot wooden fence separated the yard from the alley driveway. To the right, it divided our lot with the neighbor's. To the left, the yard ran into our two-car garage. The back door of the house led onto a small concrete patio covered with a trellis, the branches of a wisteria vine woven through it. The foliage shaded the patio and the purple blossoms smelled wonderful.

After a few hours of trimming, raking, weeding, and watering, I looked on my groomed yard with utmost satisfaction. This few hundred feet of green grass wasn't just property around my apartment, it was *mine!* Before, I had simply admired other people's yards, but now I had my own. This was our new sanctuary, our little piece of heaven. Nothing could go wrong back here.

****

Months after we moved in, we still had great pride in our new home. Even the dogs loved the new roominess and adored the back yard. And when they hopped at the back door needing to go outside, just opening the door to our fenced-in yard was all that was needed. No more leashing up the dogs. No more rolls of poop bags. No more transporting the dogs carefully down sets of long concrete stairs from second-floor apartments to ground level. Now it was just a simple opening of the door and—*voilà!*—voided bladders and bowels! In fact, I could just leave them out there to enjoy the day until they scratched at the door. We had turned one of our bedrooms into my study with a window that overlooked the back yard where I could see Dixie sprawled out on the grass to enjoy the sun. Or I might see Sparky chewing on one of his toys beside the fence. And I may see Reesie sniffing around for something interesting to eat. Eventually I realized that I couldn't leave them out for too long before

Reesie decided it was time to eat something especially foul. Once we moved into the house, he decided to take up a new culinary delight: feces.

I was looking through the window in the study the first time I saw it. Reesie held something between his paws and chewed it the same way my dad's dog Moes did with rocks. My stepmother thought that proved Moes to be an idiot, so I wondered what this said about Reesie. I knocked on the window, at which point Reesie raised his head so I could see what he was gnawing. It was a sun-dried turd.

Horrified, I pounded on the pane and yelled, "REESIE! STOP IT!" He just cocked his head sideways as if to say, "What's the problem?" and resumed munching. By the time I flew through the door, it was too late. I could see the end of the log disappear into his mouth. *Omnomnom, gulp!* His look was an apology. A nice dog, he was sad there was no more to share with me.

With his final swallow, a chill overtook my body. My hands balled up like limp claws as my arms contracted. I threw a writhing fit: "EEEEWWWW! Are you KIDDING ME? What the heck is WRONG with you, you FRIGGIN' LUNATIC?" All the dogs looked confused. Were they in trouble, or was I just working on some bizarre new dance? When I told Allyson all the sorted details, she held up her hand to stop me and turned her head aside to gag silently. That was all the info she could take.

Needless to say, poop patrol became a high priority. My goal was to pick up all refuse left in the back yard a couple times a week, but sometimes that didn't happen. When the yard had enough piles around, I had to keep an eye on Reesie so that he didn't devour too many of them. After all, when we told the vet about Reesie's back yard snacks he laughed but confirmed that they could be bad for him. Imagine that. Eating feces could be bad for your health.

Even when I thought the yard was clean, Reesie could hound down a few crusty loaves underneath the thick grass. I was surprised at his insatiable hunger for them. Actually, I don't think it really had anything to do with hunger, because he'd happily gobble down a few loafs just after eating breakfast or dinner. They were sort of like post-meal anti-mints. It seemed that he preferred a mouth that tasted rancid, and these did the trick. Even more odd was the look on his face while he ate the poo. It was a sour scowl, but he remained determined to finish what he started. The only time of year we didn't have to worry about his poop eating was when the wisteria vine dropped its fragrant purple petals. He actually preferred them to the petrified heaps in the yard. We let him eat as many as he wanted, appreciating the pedals as a much better alternative.

Thankfully, Sparky and Dixie had a different take on the brown bars. Sparky daintily tiptoed around the piles, and Dixie tried covering them with her nose whenever she saw them, which sometimes explained why she'd come back inside with one or two blades of grass stuck to her nose. Then again, I sometimes found Dixie lapping up piles of delicious dirt in the flowerbed. I thought it might be harmless, but really, why would she just eat dirt? At least Sparky ate grass like a normal dog, then threw up, then tried to eat it again. At any rate, the back yard became a veritable snack bar for our three dogs, both a bathroom and vending machine.

We had enjoyed our first luxurious year in our new home on the day Allyson and I sat casually outside enjoying a cool morning. "What's that?" Allyson asked, looking up into the trellis above our patio. "It looks like a nest."

We both got up for a closer look and gawked at it resting carefully atop twisted wisteria vines. A mother dove sat rigid inside it, watching our every move and the new commotion of three wiener dogs now looking for the thing that caught our interest.

"It's a dove's nest," I said. "She must be sitting on a couple of eggs."

"That is so sweet!" Allyson said. "You know, I've heard it's good luck to have doves roosting around your home. It's supposed to mean that you are a peaceful family and you'll have prosperity."

Another dove cooed overhead. "Look, that must be its mate perched up there on the telephone line," I said. After admiring them a few minutes, we decided to go inside so that we wouldn't disturb them. With a grin I thought how great it was to have a good omen show up at our home. Over the next few days, we took pictures and showed people that fortune had smiled on our new residence. And every day, the dogs spent more time than usual sniffing around the ground just under the nest.

Soon the eggs hatched and the nest was empty. One day I saw one of the chicks against the corner of the fence. She'd fly a few feet up into the air, hit the fence, and slide down, frantically scratching at the wooden panels. When the dogs and I entered the yard, she froze. The dogs were oblivious to her presence, so I stood watch between them and the feathery little morsel until they were finished and then shooed them inside before they caught her scent. Hours later, she was gone, hopefully to sit in a nest of her own one day.

Another evening early that summer, a storm blew through and caused a lot of damage in the area. Early the next morning, I let the dogs out and made my coffee. Usually they ran right back to the door eager to have breakfast, but this morning there was a strange delay. I opened the door and found all three of the dogs lapping at something on the ground. Sparky and Reesie were licking at the patio floor. It was the shattered yoke and shell of a small egg. There must have been another nest up there that blew over in the night.

"Ewww, gross! Get inside you two!" I said, giving them a little shove with my foot. Then I saw Dixie about ten feet away, hovering over something even more interesting. "What have you got there, Dee-Dee?" I asked.

Dixie locked on to me with her patented stare. In the early-morning light, I still couldn't make out what she was standing over, but it looked as if it was about the size of her head. I took a step toward her, and in that very second Dixie choked down the mysterious mound in almost supernatural speed: *OMNOMNOM!* Gone. Then she hopped toward the door ready for breakfast, as if her stomach could easily hold more.

I stood there staring at my open hands with my mouth agape, looking like I just dropped a thrown football. *What just happened? What did she eat?* I gathered myself and walked inside where I found the dogs hopping up and down on their front legs in front of the food bowls, ready for breakfast; or in this case, I believe the Hobbits called it "second breakfast." But before I dished any out, I leaned down to look at Dixie. She had tiny feathers all over her face and one stuck to the very tip of her nose.

I shook my head and said, "You ate a bird, didn't you, you nutball?" She gave a single, happy yip, launching a lone feather into the air, which wafted slowly to the linoleum floor. Dixie stared incredulously: *Of course I want breakfast. Let's get on with it!* I shrugged and poured out the food. As usual, Dixie finished eating first. She didn't show any signs of regret or pain at the double portion she had eaten, so I forgot about it, put them in the kennel, and left for work.

Allyson and I usually got home from work about the same time every day, but I arrived first that day. Lucky me. When I walked in, I choked on a sweet, rancid odor. *What in the world is that? Is it the trash?* As usual I heard the dogs yelping, but they seemed more panicked than I was used to hearing. I went into our bedroom where I saw them in the kennel. All the dogs piled in one corner of the spacious cage, staring me down in desperation. *Get us the heck out of here!*

"Holy crap," I mumbled, covering my mouth as I approached. But there was nothing holy about this crap. My gag reflex fired as I unlatched the kennel, releasing the frantic hounds who ran straight toward the back door. When I let them out into the yard, I noticed that the back half of Dixie's body looked like it had been dipped in mud. Some of it was dried; some of it was still gooey. In the yard, she ran twice as many circles than normal, and then came in for a landing over the grass. After a few moments of straining, her eyes staring straight up in a prayer of forgiveness, she let fly some of the worst atrocities I had ever seen. It was explosive and liquid, a feathery and foul soup. The other two dogs seemed fine but kept their distance, their noses aimed high to take in the fresh air.

Allyson had just gotten home and nearly fell over from the odor: "Good Lord! What died?" When I explained, we cleaned Dixie up, put the other dogs in the bathroom, and went straight to the vet to get the medicine we needed. Luckily we made it just before they closed, and they were quick to help us, perhaps in an effort to get that smelly dog out of the clinic as soon as possible. Dixie had a bacterial infection that had her stomach in duress, and I was sure the whole bird she ate in under a second had something to do with it. The infection explained everything except for the large lesion at the top of her black nose. The vet said it looked like it had been rubbed off, but would heal on its own with a little ointment. Other than that, he offered no theories about its existence.

When we got home, we gave Dixie her medicine and put her in a separate kennel for quarantine. Afterwards we turned our attention to airing out the house and cleaning up the larger kennel. I noticed the blanket we had in there was almost completely covered in stool. As I pulled it out, I realized that every fold held an unhappy surprise. Then it hit me (not the smell, something else).

"Allyson, come here!" I yelled.

"No way!" she said.

"Seriously, come here for a sec."

She walked to the doorway, but no further. "I'm *not* coming in there!" Then she swallowed hard and said, "What is it?"

"I know why Dixie's nose is skinned on top. She was covering her poop each time she had an episode. Look at this. All of it is buried in the blankets."

"Aww! She was embarrassed!" Allyson cooed while holding her nose.

"Looks like it. She spent so much time covering it, she rubbed the skin off her nose. Poor little girl!"

As touching as it was, we had to clean things up. Allyson let out another nasally "Aww!" then walked out, probably gagging in the living room. I got the blankets in the washing machine with a generous dose of bleach and the clean up was complete. The other two dogs could now re-enter their kennel. That night, Reesie had it all to himself as Dixie slept in her separate quarantine. As usual, King Sparky was on the bed.

Before we dosed off Allyson said, "I hope the other two are okay. They could catch this too, you know."

"I don't think they'll get it," I said. "I mean, they're fine right now. Odds are, they'll be okay." Allyson didn't respond, a sign that she wasn't convinced.

At about 4:30 a.m., Sparky began to lick my face. I pushed him away and tried to go back to sleep. He climbed up to my face again and frantically licked my nose. "Stop it, Sparky," I said and pushed him away, but noticed that he was shaking. Just then, Reesie began to whine. It happened every now and then when he heard me move and decided it was already time for breakfast. "Go to sleep Reesie," I said, and it got quiet once again. Then I heard that familiar abomination—*SQUIRT!* Somewhere between sleep and conscious-ness, I envisioned an explosion of soggy feathers, and jerked awake once the smell hit me like a sledge-hammer. Allyson drove her face deep into her pillow moaning out a muffled "Oh.my.Lord!" and a tirade of other phrases that I couldn't quite make out. I jumped up and let Reesie and Dixie out of their kennels to go outside, with Sparky in hot pursuit. Outside it became clear that they all had the abomination now. It was actually a good thing that Reesie blew first, because Sparky probably couldn't hold it much longer. If he cursed our bed with that awful stuff, Allyson might have ritualistically burned the mattress.

I came inside to tell Allyson the bad news, but she was already in the bathroom trying to keep from vomiting. When I walked into the bedroom, I saw why. Reesie's abomination had gushed beyond the kennel, through the bars, and nearly across Allyson's regular pathway to the bathroom. "I had to jump over it!" she said between gags. I cupped my hand over my nose and mouth and started planning out my morning, which included calling the vet, putting each dog into his/her own quarantine kennel, and buying a big bottle of bleach.

And that was the event I have dubbed the Great Stomach Bug of '08. Call us mean-spirited all you want, but after those days of misery, we do everything we can to keep doves away from our house. We're luckier without them.

IT'S JUST A DOG

Around the time of the great and terrible stomach abomination, I began working on my doctorate in Old Testament, and my routine as an early riser continued. I'd get up, take care of the dogs, pour a cup of coffee, and read over material at my desk while three dogs covered my feet like a living blanket. Sometimes Dixie got restless and stared at me for minutes on end. Once I made eye contact, she'd bark and hop: *Let's play, you geek!* I couldn't resist the stare-bark combination and collapsed to the floor to play with them all at least a few minutes. Later, covered in dog fur, I'd return to the books.

At my desk, I'd cringe sometimes at the stories of betrayal, mistreatment, and torture found in the Old Testament. They certainly made for interesting reading, and whether a person sees them as historical or not, the portrayals of mankind's cruelty often paralleled modern-day news reports. Part of the moral, it seemed, was that all humans were capable of both great good and great evil. Of course animals were also mistreated in those ancient narratives. I had trouble studying about animal sacrifices, but accepted the fact that it was a common practice for most, if not all ancient societies. Yet I was encouraged to find some texts that required a more dignified relationship with animals. For example, Moses' Law dictated that animals should do no work on Saturday. It was part of a divine labor law giving everyone and everything a day off each week. A proverb also stated that a good person showed care and concern for the animals he owned. Even in a society where animal sacrifice was common, there was some indication that animal suffering was unacceptable. I have heard some say, "What's the big deal? They're just animals!" Yes, they are. But even some ancient societies recognized that they should be treated with a measure of respect. Though animals were a major part of the ancient economy, they represent more than monetary value.*

I took comfort in that idea some mornings while the dogs covered my feet. I couldn't understand why anyone would willingly and gleefully hurt an animal or let it suffer indefinitely. I may have threatened my dogs all the time, but I never injured them. And really, my threats were always empty. Besides, they only yipped with delight when I said I might drop them off at the sausage factory. That happened a lot. They always loved it. Stupid dogs.

Even though they were "just dogs," Allyson and I cared a great deal for our three Dachshunds. It amazed me as I thought of how I used to be someone almost indifferent to dogs, especially the small ones. Actually, I used to believe that dogs, and really all animals, didn't experience pain the way humans did. But now, I didn't know what I would do if one of my dogs got hurt, which is why I felt pretty helpless when Sparky injured his back.

Though he paraded around as the alpha dog everywhere he went, Sparky was actually a big fat chicken. If a large dog came around, he'd have to give some growls to let it know who was boss. Once the intruder left, Sparky's tail would tuck and he'd jump into Allyson's arms with wilted ears: *Don't tell anybody, but that was absolutely terrifying!* Or he might go under the bed, his man cave, until his blood pressure came down. I think he was more interested in pretending to be tough so that he wouldn't lose his alpha status in public. Years earlier, I would have thought that made him a wimp; but now that I was older, I found that it was no different than the actions of most alpha men. How a man or dog acts is 90% of the alpha's game.

Seeing Sparky tiptoe around the house with wilted ears and tucked tail wasn't a new phenomenon. But one day Allyson noticed that he wouldn't jump up onto the couch to sit with us. A prickly streak of fur stood halfway up his arched back. Allyson's therapy skills came in handy as she gave him the best dog examination she could.

"I think he's strained his back," she said. "He winces and groans a little right around here." She pointed to one of his vertebrae where she lightly pinched. A visit to the vet confirmed her suspicions. Sparky had a bulged disk, but luckily it hadn't ruptured, so no permanent damage had been done.

"You were lucky," the vet told us as he scratched Sparky under his neck. "Dachshunds are prone to have back problems. Hopefully he can heal with medicine and resting in the kennel. We'll re-evaluate after that. Usually the recovery time takes care of things, so I wouldn't worry."

"What will happen if he get's worse, Doc?" I asked. Why do I always ask for the bad news?

"Well remember, we're not there yet, but if he gets worse, then the next step might be surgery. But I think we caught it early enough to take care of things. At this point, surgery isn't needed."

So for the next ten days, we confined Sparky to a small travel kennel where he could rest all day and night, coming out only to go potty and to eat (don't tell anyone, but we held him on our laps a little, too). Normally, he would find staying in the kennel all day intolerable, but we had him on enough pain medicines, muscle relaxers, and anti-inflammatory pills to help him forget that he was in a kennel, or that he had a back injury, or that he was a dog. Seeing Stoner Sparky on muscle relaxers was both sad and hysterical. Normal Sparky could spend an hour chewing on a ball or licking between the claws on his front paws. Stoner Sparky spent an hour just staring at his paws. While on the dope, he didn't look at me as much as he looked past me, like he was staring into my soul, dude. One day, Allyson called me sounding worried. She took Sparky out of his infirmary kennel and carefully placed him on the grass so he could do his business. He did, and then looked at our gas grill...and looked...and looked. He was frozen in a trance swaying back and forth, a little drool coming from his jowl as he stared down the big silver box.

"Maybe we should lower the muscle-relaxer dose," I suggested.

Allyson chuckled, "I think that's a good idea."

Though the dose was a little high, it made Sparky forget about the pain so that when he wasn't seeing visions of Jerry Garcia cooking magic hotdogs on our silver grill of happiness, he could just sleep. Sure enough, after ten days of resting in that kennel, he had healed well. A few weeks later, he was good as new.

All of our dogs were now mature, and Sparky was moving into his senior years. His injured back scared us enough to make some changes around the house. The main one had to do with jumping. Instead of letting the dogs jump down off of the couch and bed, we would lower them down on our own. Instead of jumping up, it was the jumping down off of furniture that put the most stress on the dogs' backs, so we kept an eye out for that. I even built a ramp they could use to get on and off the couch, even though they didn't care to use it. And, I must confess, we hadn't taken the dogs on the number of walks that they had years before, so we took them on more to strengthen their backs. It was also time to switch to light dog food. Sparky's athletic metabolism kept him trim, but the other two fatties needed to lose a little off their bellies. They weren't terrible, but the more weight in the middle made for more stress on their backs. We did everything possible to make sure everyone's back was in the best shape, which was why my heart sank to the floor when I opened the kennel gate one morning and Reesie couldn't move.

When I got out of bed, I first lowered Sparky to the floor, then opened the kennel gate to let the other two out. Dixie ran out and headed for the food dishes, and I had just made it to the kitchen when I realized that Reesie wasn't with us. I went back and turned on the light to find Reesie halfway out of the kennel, his rump sitting inside and front paws standing on the carpet just outside the gate. His wide eyes were happy, but his ears wilted.

"What's wrong?" Allyson asked, wondering why I'd dare turn the lights on before 6 a.m.

"It's Reesie," I said. "He can't move."

"What?" Allyson jumped up and helped me evaluate. With some coaxing, Reesie could walk, but after about a foot or so, his back legs lost all power. I picked him up and gently laid him on the grass outside so he could try to do his business like the other two. He didn't make his normal full circles—he couldn't— but he still was able to relieve himself. Then he tried to fumble his way inside to eat. After several attempts, he looked at me as if to say, "There's some kind of problem here." One thing was certain: his appetite was doing just fine. He ate all of his food and licked his dish clean.

Needless to say, Reesie's partial paralysis had us worried. Sparky could still get around with his back injury, but Reesie was virtually immobile. He just woke up with malfunctioning legs. But even though he wasn't getting around well, his gaze was happy and bright. Only about six years old, he was still pretty young, but a back problem that kept him from walking could spell big trouble for his future.

When we reached the clinic, the vet gave us the bad news. It was likely that Reesie had ruptured a disk in his back, which was pinching his spinal cord. Left untreated, it would get worse and maybe keep him from urinating or defecating. At that point, putting him down might be the only option. As for treatment, there were two possibilities. We could place him on kennel rest with even more happy-happy-stare-at-the-grill-while-drooling pills than Sparky took, or either he needed surgery and would likely get the same kinds of pills. Neither choice came with any guarantees, but the vet recommended surgery since it gave Reesie the best chance for a full recovery.

"Since his back is already damaged," he said, "it is quite likely that he'd move it the wrong way and damage the spinal cord even more. Worse, he could sever it completely with just a simple move. In surgery, we will fuse the two vertebrae together, making it very hard for that to happen. And if all goes well, his back will be even stronger than before."

"All right," I said. "But I guess we're still trying to figure out how this even happened. He just woke up this way. I don't see how he could have gotten injured."

"This is a very common problem for Dachshunds, and even though injuries can cause the damage, sometimes it just happens on its own. Oftentimes, it's totally unpredictable." He pointed to the table Reesie sat on and continued, "I've even had a dog standing on this table that was in here for a routine check-up. During an examination, his back went out for no reason at all, and unfortunately we had to put him to sleep."

Reesie seemed to understand and looked at me with his glassy eyes, now having an *Oh, crap!* look about them.

The vet resumed, "That's an extreme and unexpected case, mind you! But the point is that we really don't know when it could happen. It's a weakness that all Dachshunds have. As for Reesie, we could do the surgery today; I recommend it. Is that what you'd like to do?"

"How much is it?" Allyson asked.

"About two-thousand dollars," he said.

Allyson and I looked at each other with saucer eyes. They now matched Reesie's *Oh, crap!* look. So I said, "Can we have a minute to talk about it?"

"Certainly," he said and stepped out.

After a moment of silence, I said, "Well, Reesie has had a nice full life."

"Don't you dare! You want to put him to sleep?" Allyson asked. "If we can do something to help him, we will."

"Yeah, but you heard him. There's a chance that it won't correct the problem. Plus...two thousand dollars? That's a down payment on a new car!"

"But most likely the surgery will work. You just don't want to spend the money!"

"No, this is a tough decision for me, too. I'm trying to weigh everything out. I love Reesie. I really do. But it's not like he's our son. He's very special, but really...you know, he's just a dog."

Allyson gave a long sigh and began to reason things out. "I know what you're saying; it *is* a lot of money. And if Reesie was in a place where I didn't think he could live a long and happy life after the surgery then I'd agree with you. But look at his face. It's just as bright and happy as it always is. It doesn't look like he's ready to go. We should at least give him a chance."

Reesie sat on the table and stared at me, almost pleading for us to fix him. Even though he was just a dog, he was my dog and was worth keeping. "You don't want to go to the sausage factory, do you?" I asked. Thinking I was offering him a treat, he tried to wag his tail, only to produce a few meager twitches.

"All right, I'm in. Let's get the doc in here and get things started."

When Reesie came home a few days later, the fur on his back was shaved in the shape of a perfect rectangle, the incision and stitches running about four inches up his spine. If I didn't know better, I'd have thought someone stuck a strip of duct tape back there and stripped off his fur. I was glad to see that someone else had skin as pasty as mine but couldn't blame Reesie for that since his thick coat hadn't allowed a single ray of sun through all his life. Despite his new haircut, Reesie healed quickly and eventually made a full recovery. Within a few months, he was back to normal, and a little later all of his bushy fur grew back. He was his normal poop-eating self. As far as we could tell, the investment was well worth it.

We all got along fine for another year and a half before the back troubles returned. One afternoon, I heard Dixie barking in the kitchen. Of course, it wasn't uncommon to hear her complaining that dinnertime hadn't come soon enough. I could see her from the living room.

"Come here little Dee-Dee!" I said. "It isn't time for dinner, yet." She started to move: *Hi yo, Silver! AwaooOOWWW!* With a yelp, she stopped in her tracks.

"What's wrong, Dee-Dee?" She began to wiggle and smile, taking small, belabored steps toward me and then stopped completely. She continued to grin, but wouldn't move any farther. Then it hit me. She wasn't grinning, she was groaning. As I walked closer she sat in place and continued to grit her teeth in pain.

Another visit to the vet revealed the same diagnosis as Reesie's. Again, we decided that surgery was the best option. She too had the comically shaved back. She too made a full recovery. Though the financial investments were hefty, we felt that they were worth it. The two weenies were as good as new.

SPARKY IS THE ALPHA

Having grown up in the Deep South, I learned that many of the dogs people owned had more than one purpose. Everyone I knew enjoyed their companionship, but the mid- to large-sized dogs that I knew had other roles usually relevant to hunters. The Retrievers brought back any fowl that hunters shot; Pointers were used for tracking; and Coonhounds had a dexterity and obedience that all outdoorsmen valued. Even though my dogs were small, I was happy to learn that Dachshunds were also fine hunting dogs. Of course, they had to be trained to hunt, and the only thing my dogs were good at was eating, sleeping, and letting us rub their stomachs. We were always happy to oblige. Whether a hunter who puts his dogs to good use or an everyman who simply enjoys a dog's company, I've found that the best-behaved dogs are the ones who are loved and treated with dignity.

Later in life, I heard more and more stories about people mauled by dogs, and some breeds were common offenders. I kept a mental list of the ones that I thought were most violent: Doberman Pincers, German Shepherds, and Pit Bulls. If I saw any of them nearby as I walked my own dogs, I'd keep my distance. I had flashbacks of that nice lady we met in the dog park back in Dallas, who told us how a massive dog shook an unsuspecting Dachshund to pieces in a matter of seconds. So I pulled the leash taut whenever I saw a suspicious looking breed. Of course, Sparky would always growl at each dog that passed, adding even more tension. Thanks a lot, Sparky.

I was especially careful with my dogs around Pit Bulls, which I thought were the most dangerous of any other breed. It seemed that they were the attackers in most of the news reports I read—the grizzliest reports, at that. Even one of our police officer friends was mauled by a Pit Bull one night while on duty, putting her in recovery for months after it tore at her leg. Allyson had a Pit Bull encounter, too. She came home from her morning walk looking frazzled because a neighbor's dog went berserk and almost jumped through the fence as she walked by. All these events helped make the case that Pit Bulls could not be trusted.

But that wasn't Allyson's take. Her sister Heather worked as a certified vet tech for years and owned two Pit Bulls of her own. The first time we visited her and her dogs, they whined and moaned with excitement. Their tails wagged wildly, even their large bodies writhed with delight as they licked my hand. Still unable to accept their puppyish charm, I asked, "Are they licking or tasting me?"

Heather assured me they were just being friendly, but my comment spurred on a conversation that helped change my perspective. She told me that although Pit Bulls have a fighting spirit that comes from their breeding, the personality of the dog has a great deal to do with its upbringing and environment.

"They can be the fiercest dogs in the world," she said, "or they can be the sweetest. Just look at these two." She pointed at her two full-grown dogs playing with each other.

"It's true that they have a lot of fight in them, but they know there's no need for it here. If push comes to shove, they'll fight like any other dog. But they've been taught to be passive, and unless something changes that, that's the way it will stay."

Though I was still uneasy, Heather's argument made sense to me. Just like Allyson presumed years earlier that all weenie dogs were fat, I'd been thinking all this time that all Pit Bulls were violent. It's not the Dachshund's fault that he wants to eat all the time; it's the owner's fault for letting him. As for a Pit Bull, it's the way the owner treats the dog that determines how violent it can be.

By the end of our visit with Heather, I got to spend time playing with both dogs on the floor as if I was playing with my own. That is, until one of them ripped my arm off.

Just kidding.

****

A few months later we were ready for another getaway. Christmas Break couldn't come soon enough, so we decided to take a weekend trip to the Smoky Mountains to tide us over for a few more weeks. An impulse decision, we quickly made all the arrangements to be away a few days and come back just in time for Halloween. Sometimes it could be hard to find someone to take care of our dogs while we were away. A lot of people are resistant to take on so many dogs at once. But Allyson had a friend that didn't mind helping us this time. We had taken care of his Border Collie a few times before, so he may have thought that he owed us. But if we were keeping points, we only took care of his dog twice; but he'd be taking care of our three dogs all at once. In the end, I thought that meant we'd still owe him. Not a bad deal for him, I'd say.

So the night before we left for the mountains, we dropped the dogs off at Jonathan's place. The dogs were familiar with him already from the times he came to drop off his dog Maggie, so it was nice that they were comfortable with him. Also a plus was how well they got along with Maggie, whose desire to be loved almost mirrored Dixie's personality and her desire to play mirrored Sparky's. The first time they played ball in a field together, they had a few benign conflicts. We threw two balls, one for each of them, but Sparky wanted them both. If the little alpha weenie didn't get what he wanted, he'd growl a bit, but we'd correct him, and thankfully Maggie was indifferent to Sparky's attitude. She just wanted to play and get along. Her kind spirit made the relationship between them easy, and in no time they could walk on a leash together with no problems at all. That is, as long as Sparky could be in the lead.

We unloaded all the things we thought necessary to make dog sitting easy, leaving a backpack with their food and toys, their leashes, their water dish and food bowls, and even brought the big collapsible cage that Reesie and Dixie slept in at night. It was a little piece of home that they could all pile into at night. Jonathan and Maggie welcomed them in warmly. We all played ball in the back yard for a few minutes, then Allyson and I said goodbye and got into the car to head home.

The next morning, we got up early and hit the road. Though we had a six-hour drive ahead of us, we indulged in every one of them. The trip to a vacation spot was arguably the best part of a trip like this one. It had something to do with the realization that neither one of us had any responsibilities for a few days. The best part was that we could avoid all the calls and emails we wanted and nobody would fault us for it. We just started our vacation; we'd get back to you whenever we felt like it, thank you very much. We had reserved a place deep in the woods away from city life and didn't plan on worrying about anything back at home. As we drew nearer to our condo, we oohed and awed at the leaves changing color and talked about how great tomorrow would be when we were out hiking in the middle of all the beauty. The tops of the mountains were frosted with snow. We wondered if we would make it that far in our anticipated treks. Since we were too early to check in, we took the opportunity to see the sights and eat lunch at a local restaurant.

The lodge was beautiful, nestled in the side of the mountain which overlooked the town down below. The fellow who checked us in told us to drive behind his golf cart while he showed us where we'd stay. We tracked him five minutes up a steep winding road until we finally reached our spot. After we parked, he showed us up a few sets of stairs to our room, a delightful space with everything we could ever need for a brief vacation. Once we got our luggage inside, I stepped out on the balcony, took a deep breath of cool mountain air, and listened...to the silence. It was wonderful to finally get away from the humdrum of the city. While I was indulging, I heard Allyson call me.

"What did you say, Hon?" I asked.

"I said it looks like Jonathan called me several times, but my phone was off. He left a message, too. He said he really needs to talk to me. I hope it's not about work."

"Nah, he wouldn't do that, would he? He probably has a question about the dogs."

She was on the phone with Jonathan for about ten minutes, saying things like, "How bad is it?" and "Is he okay now?" but I couldn't make out what had actually happened. She was concerned, but surprisingly calm, one of the benefits of talking about injuries in the medical field. She finally finished and hung up.

"Well, what's going on?" I asked.

She took a deep breath, then looked solemn: "Sparky's been attacked by a Pit Bull."

"A Pit Bull? How is that even possible? It hasn't even been a full day since we dropped them off!"

"Jonathan took all the dogs for a walk today and one of his neighbors joined them with his Pit Bull. Jonathan said that while they were talking, the two dogs tied up and it was over in about a second. It sounds like Sparky's neck is hurt pretty badly."

"But he's alive, right?"

"Yes, he said that the neighbor insisted to pay for everything. He even drove Jonathan and Sparky to the emergency vet and made sure they got what that he needed. Sparky had to undergo surgery to repair the wound. Afterwards they brought him back home, but plan on taking him to our vet tomorrow for a follow-up."

"Wow." The shock was hard for me to take, but I tried to focus on the positives. "Well I'm glad he's alive and going to be okay. And it's great that the neighbor is footing the bill. Most people wouldn't do that."

We talked about it for a little while and seriously considered coming back, but we felt confident in Jonathan's efforts and the good intentions of his neighbor. Under those circumstances, there wasn't anything more we could do for Sparky that the other guys weren't already doing. So we decided to stay and try to enjoy ourselves, and Jonathan was kind enough to keep us posted on Sparky's condition via text messages.

For the next few days, Allyson and I hiked, dined, and chilled with all our might. But in the back of our minds we couldn't shake the image of Sparky with a mauled neck. Jonathan had kept us up to speed on things. They took Sparky to our own vet the day after the attack for a follow up. The vet said that everything seemed to be in order and that we just needed to keep everything covered for about a week. Again the neighbor paid for the visit and even fronted a sizable advance to ensure Sparky got all the follow-ups for a full recovery. He was a good guy.

So was Jonathan, who went above and beyond to take care of Sparky once he was injured. Once we got back to Memphis, we stopped by to pick up the dogs. When I knocked on the door, Jonathan let us in where we saw Reesie and Dixie yipping out their greetings, and somewhere we heard a muffled Sparky bark. He was alone in the kennel, his neck wrapped up in a thick orange gauze riddled with colorful bone decals. His glassy eyes suggested he was drugged, but attentive. Dixie barked out her normal, lengthy conversations to tell us about her exciting weekend while

Reesie hopped at the front door as if to say, "Okay, let's go! There's a Tyrannosaurus Rex around here that took a bite out of Sparky. It's time to leave!"

Jonathan filled us in on the details; Sparky was recovering well. He even growled when Maggie gawked at the toys in his cage. I had to ask about the attack, and Jonathan was brief because he really didn't see it happen. "The dogs were in front of us, but it all happened so fast we didn't even see it!" he said. The other dog had never attacked anyone or anything before, so I couldn't understand what might have caused the attack. But Allyson mentioned the obvious facts that I couldn't see, "Well, Sparky tends to growl at the bigger dogs, so he probably egged it on."

It's no surprise that the neighbor's Pit Bull attacked Sparky and not the other dogs. Dixie certainly was no threat, and would roll over in surrender before any conflict was possible. Reesie would rather sleuth around the neighborhood. But Sparky always cared about his alpha status and whether it took growling or even parading around in women's clothing, he would do whatever necessary to retain his title. Allyson and I figured that Sparky decided to challenge this mountain of a dog so that he could prove who was boss; and it only took a second for him to lose his alpha title along with half his neck. Jonathan said that he still growled at Maggie when she came by the kennel, but I don't think I would growl at anyone if someone nearly bit my head off a few days ago.

WE'LL HAVE TO PUT HIM DOWN

It was late by the time we got home, so we brought in the luggage and just left it all at the door. We were more concerned about getting the dogs inside. Dixie and Reesie were happy to be back at home, a safe sanctuary far away from the T-Rex that tried to eat their older brother. Sparky was happy too, but a dose of happy pills numbed his reaction along with his neck injury. Still, his tail wagged out his pleasure once he realized where he was: on Planet Earth and safe in his own home.

After giving him another dose of peanut-butter-covered pain pill, we put him in our small kennel to keep him separate from the others, put the other two dogs in their larger kennel, and went to bed. The injury and medicine kept Sparky from complaining too much about not being in the bed with us. He whined at first, but soon had pleasant tie-died visions of limitless green fields and all the balls he could chase, putting him right to sleep. Those pills worked wonders.

The next morning we called our vet to see if they got all the information about Sparky's attack and to find out how we should treat him. It had been three days since the local vet patched him up, and two days since he had a follow-up visit with our own vet. So far all we knew was that we needed to keep the wound covered for it to continue to heal. On the phone, our own vet confirmed that he had all the detailed paperwork, and that we shouldn't disturb the wound dressing for a few more days. That sounded strange, but he told us that keeping it covered was necessary for this kind of wound to heal. Removing the bandage too soon would risk damaging the tissue before it could reattach to the rest of his neck, which would cause more problems. So we agreed and scheduled a follow-up for two days later. Sparky was assigned to kennel rest and regular servings of painkillers and antibiotics.

That evening we prepared for Halloween festivities, and Allyson picked up a couple of bags of candy on the way home from work so that we could contribute to the neighborhood candy cauldron. Every year, several folks around our block came together for a casual party on a corner lot where the owner set out some lawn chairs, a ghoulish fire pit, some coolers filled with drinks, and a large witch's cauldron filled with candy. From dusk until about 11 p.m. we joined our neighbors to toast marshmallows over the fire while wandering trick-or-treaters came by to grab handfuls of candy. No costumes were required, just to show up and join the fun.

We decided to get Sparky out of quarantine for a few minutes and show him off to the neighbors at the cauldron. Having slept all day and nearing his evening dose of pain medicine, he was now bright-eyed and happy to be outside, even though we carried him the whole time. I think he was especially pleased to hear Dixie and Reesie yelp behind us, still inside their kennel. We could hear them barking even as we hobnobbed around the fire.

Sparky got all the sympathy in the world when our neighbors saw him, his neck wrapped up in the thick gauze. To everyone's delight, we introduced him as *Frankenweenie* and told them the whole story. Most of them knew Sparky, so their hearts went out to the little guy and were amazed that he could survive an attack from a much larger dog. After visiting about ten minutes, we placed him back into his kennel at home and retuned to enjoy the evening for a few hours. When the festivities came to a close, we came back and visited the dogs for a little while, then doped Sparky up and went to bed.

Allyson is the first to admit that fall is the best season for sleeping. I agree completely. The longer nights and cooler weather helped make our bedroom pitch-black and chilly, ideal for a wonderfully deep sleep. We had recently purchased a king-sized bed with a pillow-top mattress that hugged us when we slid under the thick blanket. After a full day of work and gallivanting with friends, Allyson and I kissed good-night and became comatose as soon as our heads hit the pillows.

Amid my gloomy dreams, I heard a muffled and unclear scream. Then I heard it again much louder. Instantly, it became an ear-piercing screech of agony that jolted me awake, throwing me into a trembling panic. What was that terrible sound? Was Allyson having a nightmare? Was someone shouting outside? Couldn't be. It sounded like it came from inside the house.

I tried to get my bearings as the screaming continued. "It's one of the dogs!" Allyson said and turned on her lamp.

"It's Sparky!" I said and flung myself onto the floor in front of his kennel. "Sparky! What's wrong?"

But he kept shrilling. He only stopped when I opened the kennel door so that he could slowly creep out, the fur-streak standing halfway up his back. Once out, he made his way to the water dish and roamed around the house as if nothing happened.

"What.the.heck.was.that?" Allyson asked.

"I don't know," I said. "But it sure scared the crap out of me!" Both of us were still trembling from the sudden dose of adrenaline coursing through our veins. Dixie and Reesie seemed rattled too, but started to complain that they were still in their kennel while Frankenweenie ran free.

"It sounded like he was in pain," I said. "I've never heard him scream like that. But now that he's out of the kennel, he seems fine."

We watched him for about twenty minutes to see if he'd react again, but he seemed normal. He even grabbed one of his toys while passing through the living room. So we put him back in the kennel and tried sleeping the rest of the night. Allyson and I were so shaky, it took some time to dose off. Just before our alarm sounded, he yelped again. It wasn't as bad as the time before, but it let us know that it must have been his neck.

I called the veterinary clinic as soon as it opened, and luckily got to speak personally with our vet about Sparky's condition and periodic yelling that had us on pins and needles.

"I'm very sorry to hear that," he said. "This kind of injury can be tough to get over. Several things could be causing his fits. He could have some stitches getting hung up in the gauze and dressing around his neck, which stings him a few minutes. Or he might have a pinched nerve in his neck. Is he doing okay now?"

"Yeah, he seems all right for the time being," I said.

"As long as he doesn't get worse, let's keep our appointment for tomorrow and we'll have a closer look. We really need to keep the wound covered a little longer to make sure it heals correctly. Let's increase the pain medicine dosage to help him out. We certainly don't want him to be in pain."

So before heading to work, we gave him the extra medicine and put him back in his own kennel, hoping for the best. That afternoon, things seemed much better. He barked out his usual greeting when he heard me arrive and had a spring in his step when I let him outside. He and the other dogs galloped around the back yard a few minutes and were quick to come back inside to eat. When Allyson the family therapist got home, she agreed that he looked better than he did that morning. He wasn't turning his head very much, but that was no surprise considering his injury. But we didn't want to get too confident, so we again gave him the increased dose of pain pills.

That night, Allyson had plans to have dinner with some friends. With an increased dose of pain meds in his system, Stoner Sparky laid incapacitated at my side on the couch while Allyson freshened up for her evening. Before long, she was ready and came to check on Sparky before she left.

"He's out of it," Allyson whispered.

"That's a good thing," I said. "I hope he sleeps until his appointment tomorrow morning."

"I don't want to wake him. I'll just head out and see him when I get back. Don't keep him out of the kennel too long, okay?"

I smiled. "Don't worry. We'll be okay. You go and have a good time with the girls."

With that Allyson kissed me on the cheek and walked out. The door made an all-too-familiar sound that always got the dogs' attentions. All of their heads jerked up including Sparky's who howled in anguish.

Allyson leapt back through the door to find me trying desperately to get Sparky under control. As I reached toward him, he jerked his head at me and bore his teeth warning me not to touch him, a maneuver that made him bellow even more. I jerked my hands back and watched helplessly until he calmed down. His shrieks became guttural howls and gargles. A few moments later he was stiff as a board, lying against my leg while I sat uncomfortably frozen in an awkward angle nearly sliding off the couch. I could feel his shallow breaths and racing heartbeat against my thigh. The poor dog was afraid to move.

In moments like these, we say the first thing that comes to mind. So I thought nothing of Allyson saying, "What did you do to him, Jay?"

"I didn't do anything!" I said, holding my odd posture. "He looked up and just started screaming. Look, I can't stay sitting like this for long. I'm gonna have to move him to the kennel."

"Be careful with him. Try to support his neck when you take hold of him," Allyson said.

I sighed. "Okay, here goes. I'm going to move you to the kennel now, buddy, so you can sleep a little while."

When I cautiously slid my hands under him, he went mad, biting at whatever he could reach, defecating and urinating everywhere. Enduring it all, I rushed him to the kennel in the bedroom and carefully placed him inside. Once there, he finally went quiet with his mouth agape and eyes rolled back. He looked like he was dead, but I felt an uncomfortable relief when I saw his shallow breathing. He had passed out amid all the pain. I watched him while I was on my knees in the dark bedroom, trembling, sweating, be-fouled with all sorts of his secretions, my hand bleeding some from one of his unintended bites.

I flinched when Allyson put her hand on my shoulder. "I should tell the girls I can't make it."

I pulled myself together and said, "No, no. You need to go. You've already gotten ready. Besides, we'll just keep him in the kennel until tomorrow morning, when he can make his appointment with the vet."

I walked Allyson out the door and made sure to quietly close it behind her so it wouldn't awaken Sparky, if that were even possible now. When I returned to the living room, Reesie was hiding under the blanket on the couch while Dixie tried to cover Sparky's poop with her nose. When she was done, she and Reesie went into the bedroom to lie next to Sparky's kennel.

Allyson came home just over an hour later because she couldn't get Sparky off her mind. So far, he didn't have another fit, so it looked like we could make it until morning. We discussed taking him to the emergency vet anyway to get him examined but preferred to take him to our own vet because he was more familiar with the situation. So we decided Sparky should tough it out until morning. I don't know whose dumb idea it was....

Yes I do. It was mine.

Then he had another fit around 11 p.m.

...then another at midnight.

...and another at 12:30.

When it happened again at 1:30—about the time when my and Allyson's nerves were completely shot—I caved and we took Sparky to the emergency vet clinic. In the examination room, the vet said that he needed to look at the wound. I stroked Sparky's back as the vet sedated him. I couldn't see the wound when the dressing was cut, but Allyson could. About the time she gasped with horror and the vet said dryly "Oh yeah, that's infected," the rancid smell of blood and puss overcame me. I felt like the worst dog owner on the planet. I meagerly stroked Sparky's lower back as I crumbled to one knee and wept. I couldn't believe things had gotten that bad and kept apologizing to Sparky over and over again.

With Sparky under heavy sedation, his freshly cleaned wound covered with new wrappings, we headed back home to catch a few hours' sleep: a hard thing to do since we constantly wondered if we'd awaken to maniacal shrieks at any moment. Still, we'd take what we could get.

The next morning, Ally and I took Sparky to our own clinic for a re-evaluation, enduring yet another screaming fit along the way, and told the vet about the last twelve hours. He could tell that we were exhausted, angry, and desperate for a solution.

"I'm so sorry, you two," he said. "Why didn't you bring him in when you saw he was getting worse? We could have looked at him then."

His sympathy softened us. I sighed and said, "We would have, but your clinic was already closed. This was the best that we could do. The whole thing just sucks, Doc. Allyson and I are a nervous wreck! We can't sleep while he's freaking out like this. What can we do to fix him?"

"I understand. Why don't you leave him here with me today so we can treat him? I'll call you this afternoon with an update."

As promised, the vet called that afternoon and told us that he had surgically removed the dead tissue keeping Sparky from healing, and that he was now recovering. As for the spontaneous fits, it was most likely coming from a pinched nerve in his neck. He was treating that too and would keep him for the rest of the week, maybe longer. We were glad that Sparky was on the mend, but weren't convinced that he would make it. Sparky was twelve years old after all, and if things got worse, we knew that we might have to put him down.

That thought lingering over our heads made evenings unpleasant, constantly reminding us of what we could lose. I'd see his Mo-Mo toy lying in the corner and remember how he'd chew it and thought, *We may never see him play again.* There was no Volcano Dog warming us up under the sheets those cold fall nights. *It may be that way from now on.* Still, we slept better now that it was quiet, but something inside still anticipated we'd awaken to screams. *We've taken care of that, maybe permanently.* At least he's getting the best care at the clinic. *But what if he's screaming right now? No one is there to hear him after the clinic is closed!* If things get too tough, we'll just put him down to end his misery. *But dogs don't have souls.*

As an aspiring theologian, I was most troubled by that last thought. I awoke especially early one morning because it ran through my head all night. After my normal routine with Dixie and Reesie, I made coffee and headed to my study at the other end of the house. It seemed darker than usual—colder—even haunted by the memory of Sparky's screams. My ears began to ring in the silent study as I wondered again what would happen to Sparky if he died.

Dogs don't have souls. At least, that's what I was taught and had accepted for most of my life. Humans were special creations made in God's image, while animals were soulless creatures that we could use however we wished, sort of like machines made of meat. The Bible relates souls to humans, not animals. So we should treat them with kindness, but ultimately, they are not self-conscious, which meant that their suffering ultimately didn't matter.

But experience with my own dogs for more than a decade gave me a new perspective. I had shared too many happy memories with Sparky and he had relied on me to take care of him too often for me to dismiss him as a meat machine. I felt the warmth of the two dogs now at my feet under the desk and opened my Bible to a story about how King David responded to the death of one, lone sheep. A prophet told David a story about a poor shepherd who owned only a lamb that he loved dearly. A wealthy man stole, slaughtered, and served the lamb as the main course at a banquet. David himself was a shepherd for years, and understood the strong connection between a man and the animals he protected. He was so appalled at the story that he demanded the rich man's death. Even the life of a single lamb was important to the king. Sympathetic, I nodded and read on.

I also found a text near the end of the Bible that identified the living creatures in the oceans as "souls," casting reasonable doubt on the idea that animals were entirely soulless. I even recalled that many of the images about Heaven involved animals: the lion will lie down with the lamb, the Spirit descending from Heaven like a dove, the divine king returning to earth riding a horse. Though all prophetic images, they at least suggested that animals had a role in the afterlife.

I finally considered the overall story of the Bible, which basically describes a troubled world that God continually works to fix. Even nature itself seemed to long for the day when everything would be made right. To put it another way, the world can suck, but God works to make it awesome; and people choose which part to play in that struggle. I smiled as I remembered one of my theology professors from years ago confessing that he hoped to see his family dog in Heaven one day, since Heaven is the ultimate repair of life's troubles—and death is the greatest trouble of all. I took comfort in those thoughts that morning, accepting the fact that Sparky would be okay no matter what happened.*

And Sparky *would* be okay. We kept tabs on him that week and were pleased at his progress. Another surgery and another week passed until he was finally able to come home, happy and bright-eyed. Best of all, there was no more screaming in agony, and only a small, jagged scar remained around his neck. Allyson and I loved having him between us on the couch once again, contently honking his Mo-Mo with joy. The other dogs were ecstatic, as were we. It was awesome.

NO ONE WANTS A STRAY

Ever since I met her, Allyson made her love for dogs clear. And even though I initially didn't share the same kind of commitment, she was coy enough to make sure that I came to appreciate them too, even the small ones. Years ago, Scrabble played a key role in her scheme even though Allyson still swears that she really had no ulterior motive. Dog-sitting the little Yorkie was a great way to introduce me to the idea of having a dog of our own. But I never imagined we'd end up with three. In a way, Allyson's vision of having a home with a back yard and a crowd of dogs was coming true. I hoped that having three dogs was enough to keep her happy, because I liked the ones we had but knew that any more would be overwhelming.

Thankfully, Allyson agreed, but it took time for me to understand that the heart wants what it wants. So anytime she saw another dog that was cute enough— virtually all of them—we'd have to review the reasons why we couldn't adopt another. For one, Sparky had just recovered from a traumatizing attack and couldn't deal with another dog. Also, there was the cost of dog food and vet bills, the extra work needed to care for it, and adding a fourth dog to our afternoon walks seemed impossible. If Allyson persisted, I'd pull out the heavy artillery by telling her that if we did get another dog then I would resign my position at poop patrol. She would have to pick up the slack, which meant regularly picking up a wonderful assortment of crusty, soft, and multi-colored piles of dog refuse wherever it was produced. Even if she was drunk on puppy love, that idea always sobered her up.

But even that idea couldn't keep her from rescuing the occasional lost dog wandering around the neighborhood. If we were out walking and she found a runaway stray, we'd catch it and contact the owner as soon as possible. More than once, we found a dog that had no collar or tags and kept it in our back yard until we could find the owner. After we got the word out, we usually reunited dog with parent within twenty-four hours.

Every time we picked one up, I expressed my concern. "We can't rescue every dog in the area, Allyson. What if we don't find the owner?"

She remained resolute. "Then we'll have to take him to the shelter."

"After we've bonded with him? After he's become part of our lives? You think you can do that?"

"Think positively, Jason!" she said. "Somebody out there is missing his dog. If Sparky, Reesie, or Dixie ever got away, I'd want someone to try to help them home, too. Wouldn't you?"

"Well, sure," I said. "But there is only so much we can do."

"I know. I don't think we should adopt another one either, but let's at least try to help. If no one claims the dog after three days, we'll take him to the no-kill animal shelter. I promise."

Even my threats of a poop-patrol boycott didn't faze her from rescuing a dog, but I believed she would hold to her deal. After three days, any dog that she rescued had to go to the shelter whether we liked it or not.

These rescue missions often took place around our home in the afternoon while we were out for a stroll, but one morning Allyson called just after she got to work.

"I found a stray dog," she said. "It ran out in front of my car on my way to work."

I was very supportive. "Ah no, Allyson.... Did you pick it up?"

"I couldn't help it! It's a gorgeous Boxer but looks like it has been abused. I could see his ribs."

"If it's abused, it could be dangerous, babe!"

"Well, he was scared of me at first. I pulled over and tried to see if he had a collar, but he kept running away. But when I offered him the sausage left over from my breakfast, he became my best friend. Jay, he is nothing but skin and bones."

Though I wasn't always in favor of picking up stray dogs, a neglected and starving animal was a special case. Since the dog didn't have a collar or tag, Allyson put him in the back of her SUV and dropped him off at the vet so they could look him over and to see if he had a microchip tag that would show us where he belonged. At the end of the day, the clinic called Allyson and told her that, though extremely malnourished, he was healthy. There was no microchip tag to identify him, but he was probably about a year old and ready to come home, wherever that may be. At the end of the day, Allyson picked him up and brought the homeless dog to our house.

I met them both in the garage. Allyson got out of the SUV first and then opened the rear gate to introduce me to the dog she had just named. "Jason, meet Sam," she said.

My heart went out to my new gaunt friend. He had a beautiful boxer face concave with starvation and a dull, thin coat of fur that barely covered his bony torso. Uncertain about me, he hunkered down and tried to tuck his docked tail until I offered my supine hand with a soft, cheerful greeting. "Nice to meet you, Sammy boy!" He leaned forward like he was standing at the edge of a cliff and sniffed my hand. Once he thought I smelled and sounded safe, he became like a puppy and rolled over on his back to take as many strokes as I offered. Some of his fur clouded the air as I scratched him, but he didn't seem to mind since he hungered more for human contact than for food.

After taking a few minutes to get to know him, we made our way into the house. Our three weenie dogs bellowed from behind the closed bedroom door, aware that we had a guest. With arched back, Sam heard them and let out a nervous whine, which put the wiener dogs into more of a tirade. Sparky was the most adamant of the three, barking and clawing at the door furiously. How was it that we dared to bring another dog into his home? He'd better not be messing with the squeaky toys! As it happened, Sam did find the basket of stuffed animals and began to gnaw on the first one he could grab, and when the Mo-Mo let out a *HONK!* Sparky nearly lost his mind.

After we gave Sam some time to warm up to the house, we let the dogs out into the living room one at a time so that they could see what was happening. Reesie, the most laid-back of the three, was first. Clearly happy to be ambassador, he romped into the living room and stopped about a foot away from Sam, who had suddenly gone frigid.

"It's okay, Reesie," Allyson said as she knelt beside him. "This is Sam."

Reesie's tail slowed, but didn't stop wagging. I knelt beside Sam, who was still frozen, and gently reassured him that Reesie was a friend. In the meantime, Reesie made his way around to Sam's rear and reached his long nose up to take a whiff. In turn, Sam leaned down to sniff Reesie's rump conveniently located beside his front paw. As I understood it, this was how all dogs said hello. After that doggie handshake was complete, both seemed fine with each other. Sam was actually thrilled to have a new friend, even if he was just a runt, and followed him around the house wherever Reesie went. He even tried to play with Reesie by offering him a toy, but Reesie wasn't interested. So Sam decided to get him involved by playfully batting at him with his front paws—just like a Boxer. That brought a side out in Reesie that I'd never seen before. The black dog actually snipped at him, which brought even more of the puppy out in Sam as he galumphed around the room shaking the honking Mo-Mo between his teeth. The happier Sam got, the more uncomfortable Reesie became. So we calmed Sam down and brought out the next contestant.

Sparky went even wilder when we let Dixie come out of the bedroom, and all the commotion riled her up into a nervous fit of whines. Once she saw Sam, she tried to run away—just the kind of behavior we expected. Sam was more animated now and curious at the new, even smaller dog that just arrived. He tried to walk up to her more than once, but she darted away each time. Eventually he gave up and continued to play with the toys on the floor. First Dixie made her way onto Allyson's lap, and then Reesie got onto mine, all of which got Sam's attention. He slowly walked up to Allyson and sniffed Dixie up and down while she hid her face under Allyson's arm. Then he turned to sniff Reesie, who was already tired of enduring the giant puppy.

It occurred to Sam that he was supposed to be up there, too. It took him about thirty seconds to blunder his way onto the middle section of the couch, which made the other two dogs jump down again. But now that Sam had arrived at the summit, he didn't care about coming down.

"I think it's time to meet Sparky, now," Allyson said. Dixie and Reesie misread her tone as something about food and darted around the room. Sam found it all delightful and scrambled, too. *I'm excited! What are we excited about?* In the process, he grabbed the Mo-Mo again and started honking.

Since Sparky had just healed from his injuries about six months earlier, I wondered how he would react to another bigger dog in his own house. When I let Sparky out of the bedroom, he came around the corner and got his first glance at our guest holding the sacred Mo-Mo in his mouth and ran up to him with a growl. Even though he was nearly a foot shorter than Sam, he almost looked down on the Boxer with condemnation. *Just what the heck are you doing in here? ...with my family? ...with my Mo-Mo?* Sam froze, looking like he was somewhere between fear and anger. The fur stood halfway up both of their backs during the standoff. Allyson knelt beside Sparky and I beside Sam. We both encouraged them to be friends, but Sparky wasn't interested. It was probably the same kind of attitude that got him that scar around his neck. We decided to get on with the rest of our evening while keeping a watchful eye on them both. After a few hours, they loosened up around each other.

By the end of the night, all the dogs had become familiar with each other. It seemed they had their own summary statements of the evening:

Sam: "I'm very happy to be here!"

Dixie: "I surrender, giant Godzilla-dog!"

Reesie: "You, sir, are annoying the crap out of me. (Mmmmmm…crap!)"

Sparky: "As long as you recognize that I can kill you in under a second, we'll be all right."

Though all of our supplies were better suited to smaller dogs, we made do with what we had. At night, Sam stayed behind a freestanding fence that we used when we took the dogs outside. With it, we fenced Sam in the kitchen at night with his own makeshift bed of blankets. We placed his water and food bowls several feet away from the other dogs' so there'd be no conflicts between the nearly starved dog and his three hosts. Designating his own toys was helpful to quell unnecessary conflicts with Sparky. We also had to buy him a collar so that we could take him for walks on his own.

Allyson and I told everybody we met about Sam, asking if anyone was willing to adopt him. We smattered his pictures on Facebook almost daily with descriptions of his sweet disposition. Actually, the pictures weren't that flattering. His eyes were kind and the fact that half of the pictures showed him in my or

Allyson's lap was appealing, but the rest of him looked like warmed-over death. We could still see the outline of his hipbones and ribs, and his feeble neck looked like it could barely support his square head. Plus, a stray dog like Sam could have some parasites or diseases that could cost an owner a lot of money. Why take the risk? Even though we said he came with a clean bill of health, few showed any interest in him.

On the eve of Sam's second day, it was time for a serious discussion about his fate. Allyson sheepishly agreed that after our third day with Sam we would have to give him to the local shelter. "You'll have to take him," she said. "I don't think I can do it." Sam was draped across her lap taking all the strokes she'd give.

"So you pick him up but won't drop him off? I don't think so! I think we should do it together," I said and sat down at the other end of the couch. "We've both been a part of his life, after all." Sam decided it was time to make his way to my lap now.

"Don't come over here, dummy," I said. "I don't even like you."

Clearly not believing me, he laid his head on my left thigh. After a moment, he put his lanky right arm across my lap. Then his left arm. Then he slowly scooted his way onto my lap, inch by inch, until I was nearly drowning in Boxer. Sam didn't understand that a nearly full-grown Boxer was not the best lap dog, especially since he was now rapidly gaining weight. But he did make a powerful case in the current conversation.

"You know, maybe we haven't given Sam a fair shake," I said. "The pictures we're putting out on

Facebook are of a straggly stray dog. Maybe we should wait until he gets healthier so that his pictures will look better. He'll have a better chance of getting a home then."

"So you want to keep him a little longer?" Allyson asked with a grin.

"Yeah, let's keep him a few more days. He really is a great dog. I think we should give him more of a chance to find a good home."

A few more days turned into a week. During that time, the other dogs began to get used to Sam. Dixie no longer spontaneously surrendered whenever he came around. But she was still careful to know where he was at all times. Reesie got the closest to Sam, and would actually lie beside him to take naps. He found that Sam had a lot to offer. Maybe it had something to do with the size of Sam's poop left in the back yard, which Reesie always tried to sample. Sparky stayed aloof, not wanting to challenge a dog that reminded him of the one who gave him his scar, and not willing to be passive either. He'd continue to growl out warnings to Sam, even though Sam didn't care to be the alpha dog. He was just happy to have a home and a family, even if just for a little while.

About the middle of the second week we began to lose hope, until one of our friends saw our pleas on Facebook. She told us about a family she knew who already owned a Boxer and might be interested in another. Elated, we contacted them and scheduled a time for them to visit us. I was impressed that everyone in the family came over: Dad, Mom, and the three kids. Since they were looking for a family dog, they knew the whole family should see what Sam was like.

They were animal lovers, for sure; and just as we predicted, they all loved Sam. Only the dad of the family wore a familiar, skeptical face. I knew it well, because I had worn the same look many times when I went to check out a new dog with Allyson. He asked all the right questions about where Sam came from and how he behaved in the house and around other dogs. After we spent a few minutes finding out about them and the dog they already owned, his face brightened up; especially when his kids began to talk about where they could place Sam's bed at home and how much fun it would be to play with him in their big back yard.

Within the hour, Sam accompanied his new family out the front door. They agreed to take him for a week as a try-out and would contact us if things didn't work (they never did). Allyson and I both said our goodbyes to Sam and his family and watched them drive away. For a second, Sam showed concern that he was leaving, but the kids covered him with so much attention and love, it drowned out all his doubts. We felt a strange mix of emotions as they disappeared around the corner. More than anything, we were happy that Sam had found a new home.

When we went back inside, we unleashed the hounds from their kennel. They searched diligently for Sam and the mysterious voices they heard a few minutes ago. All seemed relieved that Sam was gone, but we were confident that if he had stayed longer, they would have genuinely missed him. It got us thinking about what would have happened if we couldn't find Sam a home. How many stray dogs as great as Sam ended up in a shelter? We decided that we should get our next dog from a shelter. There are far too many wonderful dogs out there already, and each one deserves a good home.

Thankfully, we didn't have to make a decision like that anytime soon. We expected our dogs to be around for a long time.

THEY'LL LIVE FOREVER

One of my first years in college some decades ago, a crusty old English professor cracked open our anthology at the beginning of class and read a passage to everyone. The syllabus noted that we were to discuss ancient writings on human mortality and death. Not a topic that many of us freshmen looked forward to, mind you. We'd rather drink down the joys of another party coming later that evening. Nevertheless, it was time to take things seriously, so we mustered up as much concentration as we could. But the reading for that day intrigued me because it came from the wisdom writings of the Hebrew Bible: Ecclesiastes 12. It was a beautiful appeal to remember the Creator before the moon and stars became dim, before the people grinding grain for bread disappeared, before strong men became weak, before the sounds of birds grew faint and the leaves on the tree became silvery.

I thought it addressed the end of the world, but the professor told us that these images represented things that happened to people when they got old. An elderly person will lose eyesight and the ability to simply gaze at the beauty of the moon and stars. The missing grinders exemplify how people lose their teeth in their old age, making it hard to eat even the simplest of foods. Our backs arch and our once strong arms tend to stoop to the ground in our senior years. An old man can no longer hear the sweet and simple song of a bird singing in the morning; and unless we use plenty of dye, the hair on our heads will eventually turn gray.

"We all will get old one day," the old professor said. "And when that happens, you won't be able to enjoy those things you used to love. And eventually, even your life will come to a close. So, get out there and live life to the fullest before you can't!"

Suddenly, this became a lesson that all the freshmen could embrace. Many of us cheered and wooed until the professor told us that responsible work in school was also necessary for a full life. Way to be a stick-in-the-mud, prof!

To this day, that passage is still one of my favorites. It tells me that life is for living, and I should enjoy as much of it as I can before my body begins to break down and finally expires. This kind of joyous living is linked to an awareness of the divine. Hearing the birds' songs in the morning is a good thing, and may even point to a Creator. But regardless of one's view of God, such a passage calls us all to enjoy life before it is too late. Enjoy the sights. Enjoy the sounds. Enjoy the tastes. Enjoy people. Enjoy animals. Indulge in the experiences that they all bring before things come to a close.

Even good things come to an end, but other doorways sometimes open. After a few years, I finally earned my doctorate, and in the process I finished teaching at the private school and began leading college classes. These days I spend much of my time writing, which means I still have my morning rituals. I get up, take the dogs out and feed them, make coffee, and sit at my desk with three wiener dogs lying at my feet. Recently it occurred to me how much those dogs have influenced and enriched so much of my life. I'm glad Allyson was persistent with me all those years ago when I said that I didn't want a dog.

Above all, each dog has shown me unconditional love and acceptance, things that can't really be measured or appreciated without personal experiences. After a hard day at work, I can't help but smile when I see all three of them overjoyed to see me. That's especially true of Dixie who would bark out all of the details from her exciting day whether I wanted to hear it or not. They provide more than a physical warmth when they are all fighting to get on my or Allyson's lap while we watch a movie on a cold winter evening. When they all get a hankering to play and call me to come down to the floor and join them, it's hard to be annoyed. They're just dogs; but they are my dogs and they want to spend time and interact with me. That's pretty darn special.

These experiences make it hard for me to see them as "just dogs." I'd rather consider them a part of my family. And like family, Allyson and I have an emotional connection with them that is full of youth and vitality. Maybe it's childish, but we hope it will never end.

But the hard truth is that we are both aging, and the dogs have aged faster. The strong men are stooping ever lower. Reesie and Sparky have gotten slow in their age. Sparky is no longer the red lightning bolt that chases a ball across a field; he tires of it more quickly these days, too. Dixie's speed is about the same, and her body still runs sideways from here to there. Reesie's awkward shaped legs have become stiff, making him move around more slowly. He even has a series of fatty tumors that keep developing all over his body. So far they are all benign but emblem-atic of his old age.

The grinders at the mill are disappearing. Reesie has had some teeth pulled because of his bad eating habits, and the other dogs are on the verge of losing some, too. We're told that Dachshunds have a hard time with their teeth, which are hard to keep clean because they are so close together. But really, how much poop can a dog eat before his teeth begin to fall out? So we get them cleaned and try to brush them everyday now.

The moon and the stars grow dim. Even in direct sunlight, Sparky has begun to have trouble finding his ball when we throw it. I've heard that dogs don't have terrific sight anyway, but his has gotten worse over the years. I see a gloominess in all of their eyes, which grows denser each year.

The leaves on the tree become silvery. Dixie, the biggest worrier of the bunch, greyed up more than the other two dogs just after Sparky recovered from his neck injury. But Sparky's face and paws are now salted with grey fur, too. Reesie's chin whiskers are just beginning to turn.

The dogs aren't the only ones feeling the influence of age. Allyson and I both have grey hair coming in, and we confess that we are not as strong as we were a decade ago. My glasses prove that I can't see as well as I used to, and I'm quite pleased that my dentist keeps my grinders working at the mill. Age has made both of us a little slower and a little noisier. One morning while at my desk, Allyson snuck up to surprise me, but her joints were stiff and popped at every step she took. I spun around wearing a smile. The jig was up.

"Dang it!" she said with a grin. "I can't surprise you anymore! My joints are popping too much."

I laughed. "You're gettin' old there, lady!"

"Look who's talking, you old coot!"

She gave me a kiss and sat on the floor, only to be deluged by three happy old Dachshunds. I watched it all from my chair until Dixie looked at me and barked: *Get down here and play with us, you nerd!* So I jumped down and attacked her with a barrage of rubs and ear tugs that sent her scrambling, which got the other dogs involved too. After a few minutes of play, I sat next to Allyson who had her hand on Reesie rolling one of his tumors between her fingers.

She sighed. "Here's another one."

I reached over to feel it and said, "Yeah, they just keep popping up, don't they? He gets them so fast these days. I wonder if they will ever become a health problem."

"Let's not talk about it. You know, it's going to be a beautiful day today. We should take the dogs to the park."

"That's a great idea, Hon," I said. "We've got some errands we have to run. We could take them later this afternoon."

"Why don't we go ahead and take them now? I'm not sure when the park closes today, and I'd hate to get there too late."

I thought back to my old professor and smiled, "I agree completely. Let's get going!"

Allyson and I enjoyed most of the day at the park, letting Sparky, Reesie, and Dixie have as much fun as they pleased. We didn't know when closing time would come, but we were determined to enjoy every minute until it did.

Notes

For my fellow nerds who might be interested and because I just can't help myself, I've provided these brief notes with citations relevant to some of my thoughts. For serious academic considerations of each, you might need a book that doesn't even mention weenie dogs.

* <u>He's a Natural Guard Dog</u>: Psalm 22:16 and 59:6 relate evil people to vicious dogs that surround the good guy. The story of David and Goliath is found in 1 Samuel 17. Goliath insults David by calling him a dog along with a litany of curses in verse 43. It may have been even more debasing to call someone a "dead dog" (2 Samuel 16:9). The Apostle Paul called his opponents dogs in Philippians 3:2. Jesus says not to give what is holy to dogs in Matthew 7:6. Jesus may have been referring to pets in Mark 7:27-28.

* <u>They Are Picky Eaters</u>: The parable of the rich man and Lazarus is found in Luke 16:19-31. The dogs licking those delicious, runny sores are found in verse 21. The adage of a dog returning to his own vomit is found in Proverbs 26:11 and is quoted in 2 Peter 2:22. The corpse of the evil queen Jezebel was left exposed so that the dogs could eat it (2 Kings 9:10, 36). Dogs also eat corpses in Jeremiah 15:3. For all of these nasty references, you're welcome.

* <u>He Can't Reach It</u>: In the Standard version of the Gilgamesh Epic, this phrase is found on tablet 11

around line 116 (I told you I was a nerd!). The Epic tells one of the most popular versions of the ancient flood story. Apparently, the flood was so terrifying it even made the gods shiver like little dogs who just ate their daddy's donut holes. I promise, that's what it says. The cuneiform text is very specific. (Geez, I *am* a nerd!)

* It's Just a Dog: The "divine day off" that also applied to animals is found in Exodus 20:10. Exodus 23:11-12 and Leviticus 25:1-7 indicate that they also got a whole year off every seventh year! ...or should have. A good man who treats his animals well is found in Proverbs 12:10.

* We'll Have to Put Him Down: The prophet Nathan confronted David with the story about the lamb in 2 Samuel 12:1-5. Though Nathan wasn't really talking about sheep, it suggests just how passionate the shepherd king was about one lamb. One of the curses in Revelation 16:3 tells of a plague that kills every living soul in the sea, which includes animal life (the Greek word for "soul" is used). As for images relating to Heaven, the lion and other ferocious animals lie down with more docile creatures in Isaiah 11:6. The spirit of God came down from Heaven like a dove in Matthew 3:16, Mark 1:10, Luke 3:22, and John 1:32. The king from Heaven riding on a horse is found in Revelation 19:11. For the idea of nature longing for a day when all things are made right, see Romans 8:19